The Shakespeare H.

THE SHAKESPEARE HANDBOOKS

Series Editor: John Russell Brown

PUBLISHED

| | |
|---|---|
| John Russell Brown | *Hamlet* |
| John Russell Brown | *Macbeth* |
| Paul Edmondson | *Twelfth Night* |
| Bridget Escolme | *Antony and Cleopatra* |
| Kevin Ewert | *Henry V* |
| Margaret Jane Kidnie | *The Taming of the Shrew* |
| Christopher McCullough | *The Merchant of Venice* |
| Paul Prescott | *Richard III* |
| Lesley Wade Soule | *As You Like It* |

FORTHCOMING

| | |
|---|---|
| Roger Apfelbaum | *Much Ado About Nothing* |
| John Russell Brown | *King Lear* |
| David Carnegie | *Julius Caesar* |
| Trevor Griffiths | *The Tempest* |
| Stuart Hampton-Reeves | *Measure for Measure* |
| Ros King | *The Winter's Tale* |
| James Loehlin | *Henry IV* |
| Edward L. Rocklin | *Romeo and Juliet* |
| Martin White | *A Midsummer Night's Dream* |

The Shakespeare Handbooks

# *Henry V*

Kevin Ewert

First published 2006 by
PALGRAVE MACMILLAN
Houndmills, Basingstoke, Hampshire RG21 6XS and
175 Fifth Avenue, New York, N.Y. 10010
Companies and representatives throughout the world

PALGRAVE MACMILLAN Is the global academic imprint of the Palgrave Macmillan division of St. Martin's Press, LLC and of Palgrave Macmillan Ltd. Macmillan® is a registered trademark in the United States, United Kingdom and other countries. Palgrave is a registered trademark in the European Union and other countries.

ISBN-13: 978–1–4039–4076–6   hardback
ISBN 10: 1–4039–4076–2        hardback
ISBN-13: 978–1–4039–4077–3   paperback
ISBN 10: 1–4039–4077–0        paperback

This book is printed on paper suitable for recycling and made from fully managed and sustained forest sources.

A catalogue record for this book is available from the British Library.

A catalog record for this book is available from the Library of Congress.

10   9   8   7   6   5   4   3   2   1
15  14  13  12  11  10  09  08  07  06

Printed in China

# Contents

# General Editor's Preface

The Shakespeare Handbooks provide an innovative way of studying the theatrical life of the plays. The commentaries, which are their core feature, enable a reader to envisage the words of a text unfurling in performance, involving actions and meanings not readily perceived except in rehearsal or performance. The aim is to present the plays in the environment for which they were written and to offer an experience as close as possible to an audience's progressive experience of a production.

While each book has the same range of contents, their authors have been encouraged to shape them according to their own critical and scholarly understanding and their first-hand experience of theatre practice. The various chapters are designed to complement the commentaries: the cultural context of each play is presented together with quotations from original sources; the authority of its text or texts is considered with what is known of the earliest performances; key performances and productions of its subsequent stage history are both described and compared. The aim in all this has been to help readers to develop their own informed and imaginative view of a play in ways that supplement the provision of standard editions and are more user-friendly than detailed stage histories or collections of criticism from diverse sources.

Further volumes are in preparation so that, within a few years, the Shakespeare Handbooks will be available for all the plays that are frequently performed and studied.

**John Russell Brown**

# Preface

Trying to write about theatre is an ongoing project of varying enthusiasms and frustrations for me. Written words often seem decidedly earthbound and unnecessarily confusing compared with the moments of perfect clarity and depth that occur during a great theatrical experience, or even with those compelling if tentative flashes of intuition that drive creation in the rehearsal room. But material as good as *Henry V* is worth imagining and re-imagining, interrogating and debating, even outside its proper home and first language. Hopefully, something of the power and possibilities of the medium survives in the 'translation' that follows.

Thanks to: the University of Pittsburgh at Bradford; Stanley Wells; Jill Levenson; all the good people who used to work with the Unseam'd Shakespeare Company in Pittsburgh where, from 1997 to 2003, I really cut my teeth in understanding how to stage plays from this period; Wendy Taylor; and Jay O'Berski. Special thanks as well to students from my Shakespearean Performances class for letting me try ideas, notions and inspirations out on them.

A huge debt of gratitude is due to the Series Editor, John Russell Brown, for giving me this opportunity and then guiding me through it with a wonderful combination of patience, tough questions and good sense.

K.A.E.

# 1 The Texts and Early Performances

## Texts

Before any modern editors can give you *Henry V*, they have to decide what to do about two other plays: *The Chronicle History of Henry the Fifth, with his battle fought at Agincourt in France. Together with Ancient Pistol* published in 1600, and *The Life of Henry the Fifth* published in 1623. The first is a single volume, without 'By William Shakespeare' anywhere on it, but with a line about its playhouse life with Shakespeare's company: 'As it hath been sundry times played by the Right honorable the Lord Chamberlain his servants.' The second appears in a larger volume entitled *Mr. William Shakespeare's Comedies, Histories and Tragedies,* the collected works assembled after Shakespeare's death by members of his company. No handwritten manuscript with Shakespeare's signature at the bottom exists, only two texts printed at different times, for different reasons. The Quarto and Folio, as these two texts are called, are not the same. In many striking ways, they aren't even close.

The Folio version (F) is more than twice as long as the Quarto version (Q) – about 3381 lines to 1622. F has a prologue, epilogue and four Chorus speeches (and a Chorus character) not in Q; the first scene in F between the two clerics is not in Q; the Salic Law speech and follow-up arguments for war are much longer in F than in Q; Henry's rebuke to the traitors is much longer in F; the scene of Henry rallying his troops before Harfleur – the 'Once more unto the breach' speech – is not in Q; Q has Gower and Fluellen talking briefly about problems with the mines, while F has two other characters not in Q – Jamy and MacMorris – and a long argument amongst the four of them; F has two scenes with the French lords before the battle of Agincourt, Q only one; on the eve of Agincourt, Henry has a long soliloquy followed by a prayer, in F, and only the prayer in Q; and after the battle, F has a long speech by Burgundy about the devastation France has suffered, a much lengthier wooing between Henry and Catherine, and an extended sequence of sexual puns on love and war between Henry and Burgundy that are not found in Q. There are also many places where the content of speeches and scenes is similar in Q and F, but the exact words aren't. The differences to account for length are easy enough to spot, but what to call those differences involves making a judgement about the relationship of the two texts: does Q intentionally cut parts of F, or is Q inadvertently missing parts of F?

Many editors think that Q is a 'memorial reconstruction' of Shakespeare's play by actors who were in one of the first productions. The actors involved – the candidates or culprits are thought to be those who played Essex, Gower and Pistol – took not a script but the contents of their heads to a printer to transcribe the play. What is more debatable is what this 'memorial reconstruction' was for, and what it actually reflects. When three actors walk into a print shop in London in 1600, are they there to make a bit of extra money? Undoubtedly. But are they there to provide London readers with a great story, or to provide London playgoers with a printed souvenir of the play as staged and as they saw it? Years later, when the play appears in the Folio, the compilers of that volume seem to be taking aim at the three-actors-walk-into-a-print-shop scenario when they address the 'great variety of readers' for their book:

> As where, before, you were abused with divers stolen and surreptitious copies, maimed and deformed by the frauds and stealths of injurious imposters that exposed them, even those are now offered to your view cured and perfect of their limbs, and all the rest absolute in their numbers, as he conceived them.

Leaving aside that this 'information' is also a marketing tool and comes in a preface that baldly and repeatedly asks whoever is holding the book to buy it, how can we now know which version is the 'right' one, or which one is 'more right' than the other?

Q is shorter than F. Did the three actors have trouble remembering everything, and so by turns leave out and/or make a mess of many of Shakespeare's lines? Did they take it upon themselves to streamline the text to get to the heart of the story for this print version? Or did they fairly accurately transcribe the only play they knew, one that had already been purposely cut down from a pre-performance manuscript, perhaps by Shakespeare himself, for production either in London or on tour? Does the 'cured' version advertised in F restore what those injurious imposters did to the 'real' play – i.e. what was omitted or left out by accident as they tried to piece together the whole script from memory, including scenes where none of them were on stage – or does it put back scenes, lines and characters that the author and the company decided had to go to make it a 'better' play, either before or after it was first produced – i.e. in an abridged script with intentional cuts? And better how, exactly? Faster? Clearer? More in accord with audience expectations? Less likely to get the company into trouble over sensitive political issues? These are interesting, debatable but ultimately unanswerable textual/historical questions: Shakespeare isn't around to tell us, and he wrote for an intensely collective and collaborative medium where all of the above and more could happen, as just part of the normal life of a script in the theatre.

But these questions beg another set of questions that we can take a stab at from the here and now: what makes a good story, versus a good read, versus a good play? If we think of a story as simply the unfolding of information – this happened, then that happened, then this happened – then perhaps shorter and to the point is better; in other words, if it's a good story, tell it, and try not to get in the way as it unfolds. If we want an experience that goes beyond an efficient and linear unfolding of information, if as readers we want to take our time and contemplate things like language, imagery, grand themes and ideas, character depth and motivation, then perhaps longer and more detailed is better, as we relax in our chairs and ponder. If we are thinking in terms of what makes a good play, then our interest is in the story, and the structure and sequence in which the story is told, and those elements that anticipate the more visceral and social occasions the play will come to exist in. Thinking theatrically, we might value not the shorter, smoother and swifter, or the deep and contemplative, but instead the spiky, the disruptive and the debatable – anything that pulls us in to one side then another, that riles us up emotionally, intellectually or politically, that makes us want to cheer for or shout at the characters, or that gets us to argue with the people sitting beside us about what they thought, either during a break in the action or in the pub after the show.

The Quarto version of *Henry V* gives us a Henry who is active, heroic and victorious, just as an original audience familiar with the history or with other, earlier stage versions of the story would have expected. The Folio version of *Henry V* – the basis for most editions including the one I'll be using for the Commentary (Gary Taylor's Oxford edition) – provides a bit more than that, and certainly has the potential to inspire debate. How will an audience react when a Chorus comes out and tells us one thing, but then the action of the play shows us another? How do we decide what and who to believe when we are presented with both the official story and the backroom story about going to war? What should we think about a battle where we don't see any fighting between the two sides, but instead get a long scene of one side fighting amongst themselves, before their leader wins the day not with stunningly displayed military tactics but with a speech threatening rape, infanticide and indiscriminate massacre? A good play tells a number of different stories, points us in many different directions, and often all at once. The Quarto may be thought of as the get-out-of-the-way-of-my-preconceptions version, and the Folio as the version where the way the story gets told just might end up telling a number of other, unexpected stories.

Neither Quarto nor Folio gives us Shakespeare's definitive intentions, either in the small, in-the-moment decisions an actor faces about exactly how to say the lines, or in the overall sense of what the play means to its audience at any particular performance. Shakespeare may have meant to write a play glorifying martial pursuits; he may have meant to write a play sceptical of the political uses of warfare; or he may have meant to write a complex piece that mediates and stages the debate between the two poles. We don't know. Neither Q nor F contains a statement of intent. They are scripts meant to be performed, and so to enter into the complex relationship of performers, audiences, the cultural moment, etc. and find their place there, no longer with any authoritative guidance of what the playwright 'wanted to say'. *Henry V* came to mean things in Olivier's film, and it came to mean other things in the English Shakespeare Company staging, and it will come to mean things at the time of writing in the current debate about Iraq, justified war, collateral damage, etc. When we engage with the script's words and structure, we just have to find our way, without recourse to anything other than our arguments, hunches, gut feelings and finally our decisions about 'what the author wanted to say'.

## First performances

Evidence is inconclusive as to whether *Henry V* opened earlier in 1599 as one of the last productions in the Curtain, or later in 1599 as one of the first productions in the new Globe, but the play was written to be performed in one of the large, public, open-air Elizabethan theatres. Although these theatres and their stages were not all identical, they shared enough architectural similarities that certain aspects of the way the play was initially staged may be put forward.

Theatre audiences nowadays are used to sitting in plush seats facing forwards in a single direction towards a playing space surrounded or delimited by a large frame; when the curtain goes up, from our comfortable positions in a darkened house we watch elaborate illusions of scenes and locations move in and out of that framed area, while variable lighting ensures that our attention is directed into that world created for us within the frame. The public theatres for which Shakespeare wrote *Henry V*, and the experiences to be had within them, were nothing like this. In a theatre like the Globe, the stage was open and almost central, not framed and hidden at one end. The playing space thrust out into an open yard, and was surrounded on three sides by as many as 1000 standing theatregoers. The rest of the audience sat on benches in boxes surrounding, and rising in tiers above, the yard, again wrapping around at least three-quarters of the playing space. Costuming may have been extensive and detailed, and hand props and standard movables like a throne could come and go, but elaborate set pieces were not possible out on the stage because too many people's views would have been obstructed. The lighting in the space was variable only in as much as clouds may have moved across the midday sky above. Audiences and performers shared the continuous action in the same space and in the same light.

The proscenium arch theatre, with its magic box of tricks hidden behind the frame, and of course film and television, have conditioned us to watching Shakespeare's plays unfold rather than participating actively in them. In the type of theatre for which Shakespeare wrote *Henry V*, performance becomes more of a communal activity, with audience reaction and actor/audience interplay highly visible and, indeed, part of the show. This raises some general questions: are audiences in such circumstances more easily distracted and harder to keep focused, or are our imaginations more active, more open, and hence more responsive? It also raises some crucial specific questions: does the audience get recruited to be Henry's army, does our enthusiasm or diffidence as such become part of the meaning of the play, and are we responsive as an army of 'noble English' straining 'like greyhounds in the slips' for a good knockabout, but more complicatedly so when Henry makes us into rapists and child murderers in his threats before Harfleur? The theatre Shakespeare wrote for depends upon agreement in broad daylight rather than illusions in the dark. It encourages active participation and constant renegotiation between and among actors and audiences, and with that comes deeper investment, resistance, complicity and perhaps responsibility for the meaning of the piece as its action unfolds.

That agreement led to certain efficiencies in theatrical conventions regarding place, either verbal (we are where the dialogue says we are) or visual (a throne surrounded by characters in English dress represents the English court, and possibly the same throne surrounded by characters in French costumes in another scene must be the French court). The original staging of *Henry V* would have benefited from these conventions, and the action is likely to have moved swiftly from scene to scene with minimal props and movables: a throne, swords and armour, and flags on standards for battle scenes, an old cloak for a disguise, a fresh leek or a close approximation of one, etc. The strength of the actors' performances and the power of the dialogue would have done the rest, with audiences willingly piecing out 'imperfections' with their imaginations, just as the first Chorus in the play asks. However, the thing about a convention that makes it a convention is that we don't have to think much about it – we agree and move on. In the Chorus speeches throughout the play, attention is constantly drawn to the act of agreement between players and audiences about the story and the way it gets told. This is, at the least, a curious feature, and will be considered further in following sections.

We can be reasonably certain of the date of the first performance of *Henry V* because of a topical reference in the Chorus speech beginning Act V. In it, the Chorus refers to the Earl of Essex as 'the General of our gracious Empress . . . from Ireland coming, / Bringing rebellion broached on his sword'. Essex left London on his Irish campaign in March 1599, and returned in failure in September 1599. Most likely, then, the play was written early in 1599 and first performed in late spring or early summer. Written by Shakespeare for performance by his own company, the play followed on their earlier and very successful *Henry IV* plays, and upon other popular plays of the 1580s and 1590s about Henry V and his triumphs, and came at a time of hoped-for military triumph in Ireland. As Gary Taylor says in his Oxford edition, we have a lot of evidence to suggest that *Henry V* should have been a hit when originally produced, but none to suggest that it actually was. We don't know how long it lasted in the repertory. It may later have been performed in a touring version, and it was performed again at court for James I in January 1605. The originary moment and subsequent performance history of the play seem to be tied up in what it may be saying about war. Is it a play to rally around for its patriotism, or roundly reject for its jingoism, or does it rehearse a social debate because of the divided responses it seems to encourage? For *Henry V*, content and context are always in particularly volatile interplay.

# 2 The Play's Sources and Cultural Context

Because Shakespeare wrote for the theatre, his creations were not birthed, Athena-like, from his balding pate into this world to stand alone as singular, finished and fully-formed edifices; neither playwright nor play existed or 'worked' autonomously. The plays were created in and for a collaborative medium, socially informed and engaged, and in various ways both reflecting and creating the cultural moment in which they operated as popular entertainment. We would do well here to think of entertainment in terms of its root, *tenere*, to hold. These plays were designed to hold their audiences' attention, sometimes by giving them what they already knew and sometimes by confounding their expectations, supplying both recognizable and rich characters, anticipated and surprising action, and ideas both taken for granted and highly debatable. But they were also, as popular entertainment, repositories of how the culture dreamed itself, where fantasies of how to live played out across real if not quite accessible bodies in a communal space; the plays held and 'rehearsed' their audiences' ideologies, anxieties and desires, their place in the world, in an appropriately named wooden Globe.

Obviously *Henry V* is 'about' the historical English king of that name, but because it is a work of art, and especially because it is theatre, the play will be engaged in much more than the relation of facts from the past (although even that can be complicated and debatable). Henry is a king and a character, the action is historically based and theatrically constructed, and the time is then and now. The Act V Chorus's speech I pointed out in the previous section, about the triumphant Henry's return to London, makes all this explicit by eliding past and present, historical and contemporary figures, and former doings with current business (lines 22–35). Of course, how all these things are elided, and to exactly what purpose and effect, is difficult to pin down. How might this explicitly topical moment have been received, initially? Would the reference to Essex and his current exploits whip up a mid-1599 audience, like a reference to a popular footballer or pop star might today, so that 'the crowd goes wild' before it's told that Henry's story is even better? Was Essex already a divisive subject, inspiring equal amounts of cheers and jeers before the Chorus could wrestle the crowd back to the subject at hand? If the performance took place later in 1599, when signs were that Essex was not going to succeed, would the reference turn deviously ironic, with 'How many would the peaceful city quit / To welcome him!' being met by sniggers or silence, until the Chorus with a wry smile assured all that in Harry they were dealing with the real thing, not some upstart pretender? Was Shakespeare's writing pointed enough and his audience sophisticated enough to recognize faultlines and even critique in this passage? The comparison of Henry to Caesar brings with it associations like abuse of authority, assassination, and civil war (dramatized by Shakespeare in his next play, *Julius Caesar*), and the comparison of Henry and Essex could do as much to undermine as support existing power structures, since Henry's dramatized status as singular warrior king shows up a very real contemporary structural flaw regarding divided authority and power and a very well known personal conflict between Elizabeth and Essex (Sinfield, pp. 40–1). Elizabeth had very recently and famously boxed Essex on the ear about the very Irish campaign he was now heading (Patterson, p. 82); would an audience think of that during the Chorus's comparison, or might they already have thought about it in the previous Act when a monarch and a subordinate go at one another and 'a box on the ear' (IV.i.106) is threatened, then confirmed (IV.vii.121–2), then transferred (l. 166), then finally delivered on stage (IV.viii.9, SD)?

What is at stake here, though not definitively recoverable in intention or reception, is how the past and present moments get along. Is the reference flattering to all concerned and therefore 'safe' for Shakespeare and his company? Does it play on current martial and imperial ambitions and the popular figure of a dashing young war hero to make its historical point? Since Essex was as much rival as subject to Elizabeth, is it a subtle negotiation between the two? Does it momentarily champion a nobleman's exploits only to reassert royal prerogative and authority? And in its delivery, does the Chorus's energy run square into the audience's exhaustion over a decade of foreign wars and imperial enterprises?

The relationship of the play to its cultural context and to its sources raises many aesthetic and ideological questions, which then are informed by and tied up in the play's theatrical presentation and effect. In 'big picture' terms, gestured at by the Act V Chorus,

> We see the attempt to conquer France and the union for peace at the end of the play as a re-presentation of the attempt to conquer Ireland and the hoped-for unity of Britain. The play offers a displaced, imaginary resolution of one of the state's most intractable problems.     (Sinfield, p. 125)

Here the play as a whole may be seen to rehearse, in general terms, a current cultural desire, and it is this current cultural desire that makes the unfolding action of the play more interesting to its contemporary audience, since they already know at the beginning that the historical Henry won the day. Similarly, the play rehearses an overarching political ideology in that its action 'was a powerful Elizabethan fantasy simply because nothing is allowed to compete with the authority of the [monarch]' (Sinfield, p. 121). But in its specifics, in the way Shakespeare structures the action and the particular uses he makes of his sources, the play also rehearses all the anxieties that go along with the fantasies. The right to France so strenuously argued in Act I, scene ii, is undermined by Act I, scene i, where ulterior motives for war were revealed, and Henry's right to even the English crown is questioned in his prayer dealing with his father's usurpation and Henry's inherited guilt (Act IV, scene i). Henry's moral authority is challenged by the plain speaking of a common soldier (IV.i). Power shows itself as either violent rhetoric (in the Harfleur threats of III.iii), or gruesome if 'justifiable' slaughter (the killing of the prisoners in IV.vi) and wholesale destruction (as described in Burgundy's speech of V.ii). Ultimately right, authority, power and victory are all revealed as so many chimeras, in an epilogue that points out how everything accomplished went for naught.

Henry wins at Agincourt, as an audience knew he would, but Shakespeare leaves out of his staging of this event information contained in his two major sources, Raphael Holinshed's *Chronicles* and the anonymous play *The Famous Victories of Henry the Fifth* (*FV*). Both the *Chronicles* and *FV* make clear, at length, the strategies and tactics that allowed Henry to be victorious, from geographical details that were to Henry's advantage, to the battle orders, to the use of stakes protecting the archers from enemy charges. Shakespeare gives his audience none of these clever, resourceful, easy-to-root-for tactics, in speeches or in staging. 'Without stratagem' then, Shakespeare's play sees Henry ascribe his victory and the incredible disparity in French and English casualties to God only (IV.viii.104–10). But Shakespeare does stage a stratagem of sorts, in the only action of the battle he shows (aside from Pistol and Le Fer's encounter, which is pointedly about acquiring ransom rather than honour). Henry's order to kill the French prisoners at the moment the French army seems to be regrouping (IV.vi.36–7) leads to a massacre which (most likely) is staged for the audience. Later, Henry says it is God's arm that smote the enemy, not the axes and spears and swords and daggers and mauls and pikes wielded by Henry and his invading army but only used on stage to kill defence-less men. Is the providential fantasy contradicted by the stage picture? Would audiences take this as a complex staged lesson in how power is seen to work versus how the workings of power wish to be seen? If the play trades on a cultural fantasy of 'imperial ambition' and military triumph, it may also specifically stage the 'human cost' (Sinfield, p. 127) and ideological fissures of such pleasant thoughts.

## Sources: What's in, what's out, what's new

The standard reference book on source material is Geoffrey Bullough's *Narrative and Dramatic Sources of Shakespeare*, with volume IV covering the later English history plays. Bullough contains the entire *Famous Victories*, all pertinent sections from Holinshed's *Chronicles*, as well as an introduction outlining the play's similarities to and differences from them. Many editions of the play include excerpts or descriptions of source materials in their appendices.

The 1598 printing of the *Famous Victories* seems to be incomplete; it may well have been a bit garbled in a memorial reconstruction, and those inclined to harsh judgement might say its writing is crude and uninspired, but it's what we have to represent an earlier stage treatment of Henry's life. Some of its dialogue seems directly echoed in Shakespeare's play:

> *Hen. V*  My lord prince Dolphin is very pleasant with me . . .
> 
> (*FV*)

> *King Henry*  We are glad the Dauphin is so pleasant with us.
> 
> (*Henry V*, I.ii.259)

> *Hen. V*  But tell me, canst thou love the king of England?
> *Kate*  How should I love him, that has dealt so hardly with my
>     father.                                                        (*FV*)

> *King Henry*  And what sayst thou then to my love? . . .
> *Catherine*  Is it possible dat I sould love de *ennemi* of France?
> 
> (*Henry V*, V.ii.164–6)

*Famous Victories* tends to alternate between scenes of king and of commoners, between high heroic spirits and low comedy, and this structural pattern is most certainly picked up in Shakespeare's play. But if *FV* is a bit of a romp and not exactly a play of ideas, Shakespeare's use of contrasting 'tones' is more complex, his common characters provide as much a challenge to as a relief from the main action, and his comedic scenes have more of a sting in them. In *FV* the comic encounter of English clown and French soldier at Agincourt contains bragging, a silly trick, an escape while someone's back is turned, and ends with neither hurt; in Shakespeare the ridiculous encounter of Pistol and Le Fer is likely to end with Pistol, on Henry's orders, cutting his prisoner's throat in front of us. The scene of Henry dealing with the traitors is book-ended not with broad comedy but with the death of Falstaff, so the scene of a betrayal *of* Henry is surrounded by results of a betrayal *by* Henry. Henry's two scenes at Harfleur, where he seems to win the day through his rhetorical power, surround a scene where his men fight intensely but only among themselves. Even the comic wooing of Catherine plays out more as the continuation of war by other means, as Catherine seems to give Henry more resistance than he encountered at Harfleur or Agincourt.

One striking incident Shakespeare does not carry over from theatrical tradition involves a triumphant theatrical image for the finale. Thomas Nashe, in 1592, found particularly instructive and edifying a scene in a Henry V play he saw: 'what a glorious thing it is to have Henry the Fifth represented on the stage, leading the French King prisoner, and forcing both him and the Dolphin to swear fealty'. In *Famous Victories*, there is no indication that Henry leads the French King on stage as his prisoner (more likely Nashe was referring to yet another stage version of the story), but Henry does demand that all the 'Nobles must be sworn to be true to me' and the play stages both Burgundy and the Dolphin swearing and submitting to Henry as each 'kisseth the sword'. Shakespeare specifies nothing like this, and the scene as written doesn't really allow an easy opportunity to interpolate such striking action; as Gary Taylor points out, 'Shakespeare must have known that he would be disappointing a significant portion of his audience, and at the same time depriving himself and his fellow actors of an easy theatrical climax' (p. 28). Exactly why he did so, and for what theatrical effect, is unclear: perhaps he disliked the jingoism of the image, or perhaps he wanted to pitch an easy softball of agreement, good wishes and prosperous oaths that the final downbeat Chorus would knock out of the Globe, to his audiences' discomfort. It is certainly the case that Shakespeare's play ends differently, less easily, than the theatrical source and tradition.

With regard to Holinshed's *Chronicles* (1587 edition) the borrowings and transformations are also complex. Some of the information Holinshed supplies is simply versified and put in the play – the details of the bill the clergy would resist come over practically verbatim as does much of the Salic Law speech and the lists of the dead at Agincourt – but most of the historical 'raw material' gets reworked and re-imagined. Holinshed has the episode of the three traitors, their capture, and a stern speech to them from the King, but Shakespeare adds the trap Henry sets for them, and chooses not to make anything of the alternative claim to the English throne that Cambridge was supporting. A small technical detail in Holinshed, that the French countermining at Harfleur 'disappointed' the English, becomes the excuse for a lengthy scene of internecine conflict in Shakespeare (III.iii.1–80). Holinshed tells of an anonymous soldier who was executed on the campaign for taking 'a pix out of a church' but Shakespeare turns this suggestive incident into the struggle between Pistol, Fluellen and Henry himself over the demise of Bardolph, Henry's old friend, for stealing a 'pax of little price' (III.vi.44).

Holinshed has someone wishing for more soldiers just before the battle begins, but the chronicle contains nothing like the complexities of Henry's St Crispin's Day speech, with its mixture of calm acceptance, gentle mockery, bravado, cheerleading, social levelling, future history-making and effective team-building. Holinshed recounts Henry's order and grimly describes the subsequent massacre of the prisoners. Shakespeare decides to compare and contrast this cool, premeditated, 'necessary' action (IV.vi.36–8) with Henry's rejection of Falstaff (IV.vii.31–49), ostensibly as a credit to the king's character (in Fluellen's mind) but also to invite (or incite) an audience's judgement of both events, historical and purely theatrical.

Finally, it's worth pondering Shakespeare's most distinctive addition to his historically and theatrically based story: the scene of Henry's incognito encounters in the English camp on the eve of battle (IV.i). *Famous Victories* has nothing like it, and Holinshed has details that point in a different direction. The chronicles relate an incident where 'the king in going about the camp, to survey and view the warders, he espied two soldiers that were walking abroad without the limits assigned, whom he caused straightaway to be apprehended and hanged upon a tree of great height, for a terror to others, that none should be so hardy to break such orders as he commanded them to observe' – not exactly the way he treats Gower and Fluellen on their night-time sojourns. Holinshed's description of the spirits of Henry's soldiers before Agincourt – 'the Englishmen . . . for their parts were of good comfort, and nothing abashed of the matter' – seems deliberately contradicted by the campfire scene Shakespeare imagines with Bates, Court and Williams. These common soldiers are not of good comfort, and their encounter with the King only makes matters worse. A disguised king's encounter with his subjects may be part of a romantic and dramatic tradition, but if so it only appears in this downbeat sequence to create 'expectations which Shakespeare goes out of his way to disappoint' (Taylor, p. 42). So what might the original audiences have taken from this scene? Mostly it seems to be concerned with war, obedience, just causes and dying well. Williams raises many issues concerning the fate of the body and of the soul (ll. 133–45) but Henry initially addresses the fate of a soldier in mercantile rather than moral terms (ll. 146–57). Similes that substitute services involving merchandise and money for warfare are not at all inappropriate. Henry is a father/master sending his sons/servants on a mission for material gain; he is also a kind of merchant adventurer who risks a proportion of his venture capital, his soldiers, on this speculative deal. For their part, some of the soldiers would have been looking to distinguish themselves honourably in single combat, but most (especially common soldiers) were hoping for monetary gains, not from the king's wages but from profitable ransoms from prisoners they might take (hence the scene with Pistol and Le Fer). Taylor defends Henry's simile substituting salesmen for soldiers on historical grounds: 'in Shakespeare's age war was not yet so efficient, so comprehensively lethal, as it has since become; the risks of transatlantic commerce were phenomenally greater'. He also defends the larger distinction Henry goes on to make between the king's conduct and individual salvation or damnation: 'Henry does not deny the king's responsibility for the justice of his cause, nor does he deny that some (or even many) of his soldiers will die. But he does deny responsibility for the state of their individual souls' (p. 40). Henry actually lost more men – approximately a third of his army – to disease on the marches, rather than in battle (Keegan, p. 80), but in some ways Williams and Henry are talking past each other here, as an older sense of concern for the body's fate and its physical and moral integrity meets a newer, more mercantile, more impersonal view that sees the usefulness of bodies in the king's service as unrelated to an individual's spiritual concerns.

In medieval and early modern eschatology, a good death was one that could be observed in its approach, and for which all appropriate preparations could be made. When Williams maintains that 'few die well that die in a battle' (l. 136), he is expressing a concern that a sudden death was 'vile and ugly . . . strange and monstrous' and could cast doubts on the fate of the victim's soul, even if the victim was a just man (Ariès, pp. 10–11). For a chivalric society used to the pursuit of honour through military endeavours, a soldier's death should avoid the stigma usually attached to sudden accidental deaths, but some liturgists began to move away from that spiritual carte blanche: 'For them, the death of the warrior has ceased to be the model of the good death; at any rate, it corresponds to this model only under certain conditions: "The cemetery and Office of the Dead," writes Durandus, "are granted without hesitation to the defender of justice or to the warrior killed in a war *whose motive was just*" ' (Ariès, p. 12). The anxiety for Williams and his compatriots is that the justice or sinfulness of their king's cause is crucial to the fate of their souls, but is more than they know.

Williams's concerns also encompass a continuing popular belief in the individual's unity and continuity and a resultant fear of the dismemberment and dispersal of the body. Although some ecclesiastical writers tried to convince people that 'the power of God is just as capable of restoring bodies that have been destroyed as it is of creating them in the first place' (Ariès, p. 32), popular tradition still held that improper burial and the violation or dismemberment of the body could prevent the possibility of resurrection: 'whatever preachers may have claimed, the popular death ritual was underpinned by a strong assumption that the soul and the body were linked and even indivisible' (Llewellyn, p. 57). Fear of dismemberment is a fear for an individual's physical and moral integrity. It is an anxiety rooted in the belief that 'material continuity is necessary for identity' (Bynum, p. 254), in this world and the next. Williams's image of 'all those legs and arms and heads chopped off in a battle' reflects a deeply held conviction about dying well: that the battlefield scene of severed limbs and hastily buried bodies was a cause for anxiety, and that salvation or damnation was also thought to depend on the state of one's body as much as on the state of one's soul. 'Every subject's soul is his own,' Henry states, and while this is true, here in France and engaged in the King's wars, every subject's body is not. In Henry's line of thought, a soldier's body is a necessary tool of policy, and a king is responsible for utilizing these bodies appropriately, for their physical fate, but he is not responsible for an individual's moral or spiritual preparedness to meet that fate – soul and body are separate considerations. For Williams, every subject's soul may be his own, yet his body in the King's service is not his own, and the fate of the body is intimately linked to the fate of the soul.

Williams does talk of men who die with their sins still upon their heads, and Henry picks up on this (ll. 157–65). Historically, there is evidence that among Henry's army were many who 'had enlisted in the first place to avoid punishment for civil acts of violence, including murder' (Keegan, pp. 110–11), and so Henry evades doubts about the justice of his cause by turning war into a morality play wherein God's justice is the issue (ll. 165–76). In this line of thinking, war becomes a judgement upon those sinful individuals who fall on the field. This judgement of the individual is a far cry not only from Williams's original argument, but also from the 'largess universal' of which the Chorus spoke, and from the 'band of brothers' image Henry will use in the morning. It also raises problems if followed through to Henry's order on the battlefield the next day that 'every soldier kill his prisoners' (IV.vi.37). To free up his men and to ensure there would be no revolt from behind the English lines should the apparently imminent French attack from the front have any success, the order to kill the prisoners is comprehensible as a battlefield tactic but not necessarily defensible as an ethical position:

> Henry, a Christian king, was also an experienced soldier and versed in the elaborate code of international law governing relations between a prisoner and his captor. Its most important provision was that which guaranteed the prisoner his life – the only return, after all, for which he would enter into anything so costly and humiliating as ransom bargaining. And while his treachery broke that immunity, the mere suspicion, even if well-founded, that he was about to commit treason could not justify his killing. At a more fundamental level, moreover, the prisoner's life was guaranteed by the Christian commandment against murder, however much more loosely that commandment was interpreted in the fifteenth century.  (Keegan, p. 109)

If killing the prisoners was in any way felt to be murder outside the accepted course of battle, then we are back to Williams's concern about the state of one's soul when blood is the argument, and if it is the King's direct order that his soldiers commit such a sin on the battlefield, we return to considering the responsibility of the King that led them to it.

Williams's concern for bodily integrity is reworked in Henry's St Crispin's Day speech; here, the future wounded body is precisely the commodity Henry repackages to sell to his troops (IV.iii.44–51). Henry offers to write 'honour' in the wounds and scars his men will suffer, to memorialize their integrity in battle in their future less-than-whole bodies. This use of the body is not inappropriate to a chivalric code. But when the trumpets sound to announce the battle, there may be some in this band of brothers (and in the audience) who are thinking ahead, not to scars for St Crispin's day, but to the fate of bodies at that other trumpet blast at the end of time.

## Henry IV, Part Three?

Shakespeare had already written two plays featuring the man who would become 'this star of England' (Epilogue, l. 6), in his earlier incarnation as the dissolute, troublemaking, Prince-gone-slumming Hal. While overarching plans are debatable in terms of Shakespeare's intentions and methods for writing his second historical tetralogy (see Critical Assessments), members of the original theatrical audience for *Henry V* would have a context and expectations created by its very popular precursor plays. The beginning of the play provides a helpful gloss on both the theatrical tradition of the Hal-to-Henry story and Shakespeare's re-imagining of it. Canterbury gives an account of the miraculous conversion and reformation of the prodigal son (I.i.25–60) that audiences would recognize from the Chronicles and earlier stage versions, while Ely suggests a more calculated course of events – an educational process where 'the Prince obscured his contemplation / Under the veil of wildness' (ll. 64–5) – that links to an early and key soliloquy by Hal two plays previously. 'I know you all,' he says to his low-life friends' exiting backs,

> and will awhile uphold
> The unyoked humour of your idleness.
> Yet herein will I imitate the sun,
> Who doth permit the base contagious clouds
> To smother up his beauty from the world,
> That when he please again to be himself,
> Being wanted he may be more wondered at
> By breaking through the foul and ugly mists
> Of vapours that did seem to strangle him. . . .
> So when this loose behavior I throw off
> And pay the debt I never promised,
> By how much better than my word I am,
> By so much shall I falsify men's hopes;
> And like bright metal on a sullen ground,
> My reformation, glitt'ring o'er my fault,
> Shall show more goodly and attract more eyes
> Than that which hath no foil to set it off.
> I'll so offend to make offence a skill,
> Redeeming time when men least think I will.

> (*1 Henry IV*, I.ii.192–214)

Ely's explanation also links to a defence of Hal's character, and his intentions, given to his doubting father in the previous play:

> WARWICK   The Prince but studies his companions,
> Like a strange tongue, wherein, to gain the language,
> 'Tis needful that the most immodest word
> Be looked upon and learnt, which once attained,
> Your highness knows, comes to no further use
> But to be known and hated; so, like gross terms,
> The Prince will in the perfectness of time
> Cast off his followers, and their memory
> Shall as a pattern or a measure live
> By which his grace must mete the lives of other,
> Turning past evils to advantages.

> (*2 Henry IV*, IV.iii.68–78)

As Canterbury concludes (with a wry smile?) in *Henry V*,

> Miracles are ceased,
> And therefore we must needs admit the means
> How things are perfected.
>
> (I.i.68–70)

Shakespeare creates, over the course of two plays, a calculating Hal, whose reformation is a pre-meditated, carefully choreographed climax to his gutter education. His 'common touch' is a manipulated means to his eventual perfection rather than an essential attribute.

So what kind of man, and what kind of plan, is this? We don't know how Shakespeare's audience 'read' Hal, nor can we be sure of Shakespeare's intentions in creating him this way. But we do have some further interesting comments in the plays themselves. When Hal and his father appear to be reconciled in *Henry IV, Part 1*, the prince tells the king 'I shall hereafter, my thrice-gracious lord, / Be more myself' (III.ii.92–3), but in the next scene appears to be bragging to his companions: 'I am good friends with my father, and may do anything' (III.iii.182–3), as though heartfelt reconcilement is merely a cover and licence for more bad behaviour. Later, in *Henry IV, Part 2*, Hal and Poins discuss the thorny dilemma of what precisely constitutes that 'self' he once assured his father he'd be more like:

> PRINCE HARRY  By this hand, thou thinkest me as far in the devil's book as thou and Falstaff, for obduracy and persistency. Let the end try the man. But I tell thee, my heart bleeds inwardly that my father is so sick; and keeping such vile company as thou art hath, in reason, taken from me all ostentation of sorrow.
>
> POINS  The reason?
>
> PRINCE HARRY  What wouldst thou think of me if I should weep?
>
> POINS  I would think thee a most princely hypocrite.
>
> PRINCE HARRY  It would be every man's thought, and thou art a blessed fellow to think as every man thinks. . . . Every man would think me an hypocrite indeed.
>
> (II.ii.38–52)

Perhaps the princely hypocrite feels himself a bit locked in the role and course he has chosen; perhaps the personal cost was the only thing he didn't calculate in that early soliloquy, and is something that he only adds up much later, in another play, on a dark night before Agincourt. Hal's friends will have to go – even his surrogate father Falstaff. He does this in *Henry IV, Part 1* 'in jest' or perhaps in dress rehearsal:

> SIR JOHN    Banish not him thy Harry's company,
> Banish Plump Jack, and banish all the world.
> PRINCE HARRY    I do. I will.

> (II.v.484–6)

He does it again in *Henry IV, Part 2* in deadly earnest:

> SIR JOHN    My king, my Jove, I speak to thee, my heart!
> KING HARRY    I know thee not, old man. Fall to thy prayers.
> How ill white hairs become a fool and jester!
> I have long dreamt of such a kind of man,
> So surfeit-swelled, so old, and so profane;
> But being awake, I do despise my dream. . . .
> Presume not that I am the thing I was,
> For God doth know, so shall the world perceive,
> That I have turned away my former self . . .

> (V.v.46–58)

The young Prince Hal told us it was coming, but what is his emotional state (cool, calculated, heartbroken, numb) or our reaction (understanding, appalled) at his being as good as his word?

The epilogue to *Henry IV, Part 2*, perhaps to give Shakespeare some room to manoeuvre, is not very explicit about where the characters and story will go from here:

> EPILOGUE    One word more, I beseech you. If you be not too much cloyed with fat meat, our humble author will continue the story with Sir John in it, and make you merry with fair Catherine of France; where, for anything I know, Falstaff shall die of a sweat – unless already a be killed with your hard opinions.

> (ll. 24–9)

But if this epilogue is reticent, coy, tentative, planting red herrings or just unsure, we do get the essential action of the next sequel in two other places. Before he died, Hal's father gave him some very politic advice to avoid trouble at home by stirring it up abroad:

> KING HENRY          Therefore, my Harry,
>   Be it thy course to busy giddy minds
>   With foreign quarrels, that action hence borne out
>   May waste the memory of the former days.
>
> (IV.iii.341–4)

At the very end of *Henry IV, Part 2* it seems this advice is to be well and swiftly taken:

> PRINCE JOHN    The King hath called his parliament, my lord.
> LORD CHIEF JUSTICE    So he hath.
> PRINCE JOHN    I will lay odds that, ere this year expire,
>   We bear our civil swords and native fire
>   As far as France. I heard a bird so sing,
>   Whose music, to my thinking, pleased the King.
>
> (V.v.101–6)

We will meet this bird in ecclesiastical feathers in the first scene of *Henry V*, and in the second scene we'll hear, at great length, the sweet music he sings.

# 3 Commentary

## Prologue

**1–34**    A man walks into the playing space. We watch him, he looks at us, and then he asks us for something: if we want to get the most out of the play, we will have to use our imaginations and actively assist our presenters. We probably wouldn't be going to the theatre if we weren't interested in using our imaginations, so these terms may strike us as quite reasonable. We can't have the things themselves, but we know we're going to get a representation of kingdoms, princes, monarchs, warlike Harry and the battle of Agincourt in this history-as-play. The stage is set. We're ready to begin.

Except, of course, we already have begun. The moment a particular actor enters the shared space with us, choices are being made and responses are being generated. Does the actor stride out firmly and directly to meet us, or come into the space in a slow arc that might be interpreted as guarded or tentative? Does he have an air of authority about him, or does he seem timid, unsure? We react to different physical types differently – is the actor tall and imposing? Plump and jovial? Attractive? Seedy? Is he performing for us or addressing us openly and honestly? Is he humble, or is he sizing us up? Is he trying to pump us up for what is to come, or is he efficiently dispensing with a few preliminaries before the real action begins? He asks us for something. As we listen, does the favour he's asking seem reasonable, or does he come across as if he's buttonholing us or trying to sell us something? What if the actor is female, and it is a woman who comes forward to lead us through this martial history of battles and conquests?

Any act of theatre is a complex, often fluid interplay of choices, expectations, intentions, and responses. The goal of this Commentary

23

is to provide you, the reader, with some sense of the active engagement of the theatrical event, with only a playscript before you.

## Introduction to the Commentary

As words on a page, a playscript is both woefully incomplete as well as much more than the sum of its parts. It is a halfway house, a waystation between imaginative labour as the author bends his pen, and physical representation as a company of actors give it theatrical embodiment. A playscript has a certain permissiveness as part of a co-creative endeavour: even Shakespeare, great as he is, cannot do it all himself, and relies on the kindness – and the skills and experience and the voices and the bodies – of others who will always be 'doing things' with the script. But a playscript also contains certain imperatives: it may offer a number of possibilities but it also demands that definite choices *in action* be made, as any actor worth his or her salt knows that you cannot perform indeterminacy. Theatre is a living dialogue between artists and audiences both present in the same place at the same time, and the social event will contain not just the artists' intentions and the audiences' reception of them (which may or may not correspond to those intentions) but also something of how a society 'feels' at that particular moment in its cultural and political life. Artistic permissiveness, production imperatives, social dialogue and debate: a text for the theatre is a uniquely complex meaning-delivery device.

When reading a playscript, we have to think of it as more than just pages of dialogue in a physical vacuum. We have to imagine more viscerally, and try to keep bodies in mind, whether considering the individual actors and how they comport themselves while delivering lines or listening to someone else's, or mapping some of the possible physical positions of groups within scenes and how they then shift between scenes. In this way, we can begin to contemplate a physical narrative to the unfolding action. Certain key sequences in *Henry V* – dealing with the traitors, the entreaties and threats before Harfleur, the 'Band of Brothers' speech – depend enormously for their meanings on how Henry works his crowd, on stage or in the audience, and how that crowd responds. How we perceive certain relationships – like that of Henry and Catherine in the wooing scene – may also depend on the distance between characters and movement in response. It's important, when reading, to have some sense of the spatial relations that actors naturally play around with when on stage with other actors.

In this Commentary I'll often be considering three important categories as we read with the possibilities of performance in mind:

1. **Stage Directions**   We'll look for staging actually noted in the text and consider what is being asked for, how specific or permissive it might be, and whether there are differences of note between directions recorded in F and Q.

2. **Implied Stage Action**   This requires even more imaginative engagement, where we have a sense of what happens from the dialogue but not an exact indication of how. When Pistol says to Fluellen 'Quiet thy cudgel,' it's a pretty sure bet that a beating has just been administered – although it could be anywhere between comedic and brutal. When Henry says to Catherine 'You have witchcraft in your lips,' odds are he has just kissed her, but the nature of that kiss – mutual or forced – is not specified and yet will completely dictate our response to the scene.

3. **Performance Choices**   This is the broadest category, and allows us to consider choices that are made, either moment by moment in the acting and blocking (we can consider enacted psychological and emotional life, physical action, vocal inflection and emphasis, etc.) or in broader terms such as the kind of stage world within which any individual moment of action exists (we can imagine the physical/visual in terms of production design, use of the space and patterns of choreography). I'll be focusing less on what actors might be *thinking* than on what they might be *doing*, and so suggesting physical action more than ascribing psychological nuance. It's hard to talk about how we *should* react to anything in the script or played out in performance, but I will suggest *possible* reactions, if only to point out how and where responses could be wildly divergent, depending on different paths taken through performance choices.

American playwright Paula Vogel says that a script is not so much about words as it is about structure and sequence. I'll give attention not just to content scene by scene, but also to the cumulative experiences of how the content of one scene smashes up against and generates dramatic sparks off the scenes that precede or follow. In *Henry V* we are challenged to make judgements or take sides in the play's unfolding argument, but often the very next scene forces us to rethink those judgements and question our own complicity in the action.

## ACT I

### Act I, scene i (*Note*: all references are taken from Gary Taylor's Oxford edition)

1–21    At the beginning of the play, the Chorus told us of kingdoms and monarchs, open spaces and epic battles, horses' hooves and thousands of soldiers, and suggested that the accomplishments of many years will be packed into a short amount of stage time. This is fine rhetoric, and must at least set up some expectation of grand and breathless action to follow. But what does follow is a scene of two clergymen (who sound a lot like politicians) discussing the finer points of a bill now before parliament. If we were expecting to be transported to 'vasty' fields we seem instead to be listening in on a hushed and hurried discussion somewhere along the corridors of power. While the action is smaller in scope, it may still be breathless. They enter in the middle of their conversation – 'My lord, I'll tell you' – discuss this bill with some intensity – 'How . . . shall we resist it?' 'It must be thought on' – and Canterbury proceeds to itemize at length the damage that could be done to them and the Church. We know why the bill is important to Canterbury and Ely:

> ELY    This would drink deep.
> CANTERBURY                        'Twould drink the cup and all.

But is there desperate, bitter irony or something of a twinkle in Canterbury's joke here? And what does any of it have to do with warlike Harry and the Chorus's promised conflict between two mighty monarchies?

**22–3**   The answer may depend on a purely performative moment that follows. Ely presses the point: 'But what prevention?' This is a half-line, indicating a possible pause before Canterbury answers. On the page, Canterbury's reply may at first appear to be changing the subject: 'The King is full of grace and fair regard.' But the actor playing Canterbury has a choice to make here. He can pause, rack his brain, come up with nothing, throw up his hands and talk instead about the king. But if he were to pause, relax and smile before replying, then we would know that Canterbury is not changing the subject but rather showing the ace he has in his pocket against the bill, in the form of Henry himself. Canterbury's physical and vocal attitude here will determine the meaning of the rest of the exchange: he can be a desperate man flailing his way towards whatever course of action they come up with, or calm and confident as he hints at a plan already set in motion.

**24 to the end**   Possible justification for the latter choice comes towards the end of the scene, where Canterbury tells Ely of the substantial monetary offer made to the king 'in regard of causes now in hand . . . as touching France' coupled with particulars of the 'true titles' Henry has to the French throne, which simply require some further time to explain. The domestic bill, which the clergy fears, has already been countered with a proposal for foreign conquest that the clergy will support. Canterbury's exit lines (ll. 96–8) concerning the French ambassador further indicate Canterbury's intimate knowledge of, and possible hand in, already unfolding events. As regards structure and sequence, if the Chorus led us to expect heroics, Shakespeare instead seems to have given us *realpolitik*. In terms of performance choices, if Canterbury plays the scene with sly, relaxed confidence, then we may well be asking just who is running the show in the scene to follow, and whether we are watching a moral debate or a political done deal.

## Act I, scene ii

**Stage direction**    What do we make of Henry on his first entrance? Much depends on his demeanour – confident or nervous, open or guarded? – on his spatial relations with the others who enter with him – a man apart or a leader moving easily among his council? – and on the attitude of his on-stage audience – are the members of Henry's council relaxed or wary, formal or informal, working with Henry or observing and judging him at every step? The exact size and make-up of Henry's on-stage audience varies in the Quarto and Folio texts. F calls for six of Henry's relatives and noblemen (all named) to enter with him, while Q introduces an ambiguous 'and other Attendants' into this initial entrance. Many editions that use F as the base text add 'other attendants' as in Q; this is thought to be helpful to a reader and reasonable for the ensuing action. Some editors believe the extras are needed at line 221 to go and fetch the French Ambassador. Of course, it could be Exeter or another member of Henry's council who goes off to get the Ambassador, and this helpful addition to the stage direction could radically change the atmosphere and impact of the scene. 'Other attendants' begs the questions of who, and how many. Are we to think of the stage filling up here with attendant lords, heralds, trumpeters and the like, making it into a grand and very public state spectacle? This could turn every word and action to follow into a performance designed for a more general public consumption, whereas the Folio stage direction seems to indicate that we are looking in on the workings of the King's inner circle.

**1–32**    If we wondered why Shakespeare started the play's action with the clergy's interests and manoeuvres, then Henry's first line confirms that Canterbury and his proposition will be at the centre of what is to come. Canterbury and Ely appear, perhaps even conspicuously on cue. Canterbury offers a rather formal greeting, but Henry interrupts him, finishing the line and getting directly down to business. Perhaps Canterbury begins to answer as soon as the question is posed at the end of line 12 (after all, we know from the first scene that part of his strategic counter-offer included these 'severals and unhidden passages' by which Henry can claim France as his). But Henry proceeds past the question (and runs over Canterbury if he tried to jump in) to impose a moral frame upon whatever Canterbury will answer – an answer that may serve to awake Henry's 'sleeping sword of war'. Of course, because of what we know from Act I, scene i, we may wonder whether that sword is only pretending to be asleep, and if a plan to conquer France has already been put into motion. Again, much depends on the actor's choices in delivering the speech. Is Henry speaking with devout gravity when he uses the name of God three times in addressing this company, or is he being slightly sarcastic in charging a clergyman 'in the name of God' to tell the truth? Does Henry move through the speech slowly, carefully and forcefully, again making everyone clear on the gravity of the situation, or does he breeze through it, impatient for the answer he knows he's going to get? Henry's physical position is also important. He may be lecturing Canterbury from his throne – Canterbury's formal greeting (ll. 7–8) could be an implied stage direction that indicates there is a throne on stage and Henry is seated on it, but the line could just as well be referring to the throne metaphorically. Does Henry hold Canterbury at a distance, or is he welcoming, even chummy, inviting Canterbury to an equal place at the council table to be part of this important decision? Henry's caution to Canterbury ends on a half-line. Does Canterbury hesitate, not expecting that he would be morally so put on the spot here? Are Canterbury and Ely collecting their thoughts – and perhaps their papers – before addressing Henry's question? Or perhaps Canterbury simply uses the pause to take a deep breath before confidently launching into 63 lines of detailed historical precedent for Henry's imperial aspirations.

**33–95**  This speech may be comprehensible in terms of its argument and accuracy if studied closely, and it may be of interest for those with a penchant for, and some prior knowledge of, medieval French history or issues of primogeniture. When reading the play, we may 'get it' if we also read the section on Salic Law in the introduction and all the commentary at the bottom of the page (often longer and more detailed than the speech itself). But a 63-line speech can, generally speaking, make for deadly theatre. Why does Shakespeare put this speech here, and what can be done with it? In terms of stage

action rather than historical content, what are Canterbury's intentions with the speech, and what kind of on-stage reactions might it
provoke?

One approach is to play the speech as comic in nature, and the
comedy can be buoyantly slapstick or deeply ironic. Canterbury and
Ely can make a great double-act, with papers flying and charts opening upside-down and heavy tomes threatening to crush lecturer,
assistant and listeners alike. After flirting with chaos and adding
much comic *shtick*, the speech then has its natural punchline in
Canterbury's assertion that all is 'as clear as is the summer's sun'. The
on-stage audience can have a good laugh, we can have a good laugh
– although we may wonder for a moment if it's comfortable laughing
through an argument that will launch a war. The comedy might be
more cutting if Canterbury is a consummate salesman and so over-
whelms his audience with the speed, dexterity and assuredness of his
argument that they will be willing to buy anything by the end of it.
After all, we know that the clergy has something to sell here, and that
these 'true titles' are meant to be a distraction from that parliamen-
tary bill so important in Act I, scene i, and never mentioned here.
There may be a certain ironic pleasure to be gained from watching
someone manipulate and tie others in knots, even in so serious a
context.

If the speech is approached seriously, it might be up to the on-
stage audience to guide our reactions to get us through it. If this
really is a moment of decision on a very serious matter, then the
King's council can create and direct a strong focus through carefully
studying Henry, gauging his reactions to try to anticipate his
response. If Henry remains poker-faced while everyone else,
Canterbury included, is trying to read him, then there is a chance
that enough on-stage tension could be generated and maintained
through such a high-stakes argument to make it compelling theatre.
Even if it is taken very seriously, we can still marvel at the bad faith
involved, considering that the clergy's vested interests and ulterior
motives have already been made clear to us. Perhaps the on-stage
audience of the King's council is also aware of those motives.
Perhaps those motives coincide quite nicely with their own desires
for honour, renown, chivalric display, imperial acquisitions or some

testosterone-fuelled brawling, and thus heighten their interest and attention to the argument, its progression and outcome. One staging possibility, however, is not a good theatrical option: having Canterbury's on-stage audience start to drift off, glaze over and nod asleep may get a cheap laugh, but will be more likely only to result in creating the same response in the theatre audience.

**96–135**   With this Salic Law apparently discredited, Henry asks once again for his double guarantee: 'May I with right *and* conscience make this claim?' The emphatic response – 'The sin upon my head, dread sovereign' – is either Canterbury's most shameless assertion yet, given his underlying motives, or Henry's rather clever and public shifting of responsibility away from himself for what is to come, given his inclinations hinted at in Act I, scene i. What follows may be a fitting testament to Canterbury's clear and faultless logic, or a comic example of group-think with everyone quickly jumping on board, or the moment almost everyone in the room shows their hand and stops pretending there could be any other outcome here. If the on-stage audience has been building the tension through active listening – careful attention, quick glances, knowing looks, and silent conferrals amongst themselves – then now is their time to spring into more overt action. Canterbury shifts from legal argument to quoting scripture and conjuring (in) the names of Henry's 'mighty ancestors'. His language now changes to imperatives: 'stand . . . unwind . . . look . . . go . . . invoke'. Ely speaks for the first time in the scene, and he is equally emphatic: 'Awake . . . Renew.' Exeter adds his voice and, apparently, that of world opinion (ll. 122–3) to the call to arms, and Westmorland further assures Henry that his subjects' hearts and spirits are already 'in the fields of France'. Canterbury looks to wrap things up with, for a man of God, a particularly colourful exhortation to 'blood and sword and fire' and, finally, a reminder of the monetary offer (ll. 132–5) we heard about in Act I, scene i. The sudden urgency and sustained pressure of this exchange can be breathtaking after the Salic Law speech, whether it's played around a table or with each man in turn rushing towards the throne to spur on his leader.

**136–82**   Whether these men have overplayed their crafty hands or
just succumbed to natural exuberance, Henry meets them with
another concern, this time about homeland security. Henry's tone
here could bring some caution and gravity back to the situation, or
he might be saying 'not so fast' with a dry smile, or perhaps he just
enjoys seeing his advisors jump through hoops to get what they all
want. Henry's new addition to the debate ends with a half-line. The
pause could be filled with a certain dismay from the now overcom-
mitted company, or a smile of acknowledgement that they have got
ahead of themselves, or at least a breath while they take their seats
again and regroup for further argument. Perhaps Henry's advisors
look around amongst themselves for who will field this one, with
Canterbury finally having a cursory go at it. But Henry, having done
his historical research, presses his point about the Scot, to be countered by Canterbury, who we know by now has also done his
research. There is disagreement in the sources about the next
speaker: the Folio gives it to Ely, while the Quarto ascribes it to a
Lord. Since the speech contradicts Canterbury, for more serious
intent it makes sense to give it to one of the noblemen, such as
Westmorland; however, if left with Ely, the event of the underling
contradicting his superior could give rise to some nice comic business like an elbow to the ribs or a kick under the table. Whether the
clergy are squabbling here or one of the noblemen is momentarily
wavering, Exeter coming in on Canterbury's side seems just the thing
to give Canterbury the boost of energy and the assurance to launch
into his disputation on obedience, civil order and honey bees, which
finally concludes the matter.

**183–233**   Canterbury's speech would seek to naturalize the course
of action proposed. His honey-bee version of warfare (ll. 187–204)
with its merry march of perpetual spoil seems a far cry from the
'much fall of blood' and 'waste in brief mortality' Henry spoke of
earlier (lines 25, 28). We can laugh at Canterbury's persistence or
shake our heads at his cheerful sophistry, but by the end at least
Henry has, quite firmly, made up his mind. Whether this speech (ll.
222–33) is delivered with quiet gravity or youthful bravado is likely to
depend on the performance choices Henry has made thus far. How

Henry delivers his decision will in turn determine whether his advisors catch their breaths in awe of what is to come, or shoot quick smiles amongst themselves, or explode into cheers and congratulatory backslapping.

**233 stage direction**  There is some confusion about the size and nature of the embassy Henry is now prepared to receive. Canterbury, Westmorland and Henry have all spoken of a singular ambassador (I.i.92; I.ii.3, 5); Henry asks for plural messengers to be sent in (l. 221); stage directions in both Folio and Quarto call for plural 'Ambassadors of France'. If the scene thus far has been intimate, involving the King's inner council only, then perhaps now is the time to open things up by bringing in the French Ambassador, his attendants bearing the Dauphin's 'gift' and English attendants accompanying the embassy. In this way, the resolve and promised forward movement of the action that comes with Henry making his decision would be reflected in a burst of colour, movement and new energy onto the playing space.

**234–57**  We now get the embassy Canterbury talked of in the first scene, the message of which he was confident he could guess in advance. By this time, Henry has already made up his mind what he is going to do regarding France. Politically, the French embassy would appear to be superfluous; theatrically, it might appear as if it were going to be anti-climactic. But the Dauphin's response and the treasure he sends actually set up the true climax of the scene.

First, there are many decisions to be made about this initial appearance of the French. Are they formal or foppish? Are they a bunch of sniggering lackeys to signal French disregard of the boy-king, or are they led by one of the key French characters we will see more of later? Does the French Ambassador bow to one of the English Lords instead of the King, either as bumbling slapstick or as coolly calculated insult? What holds the Dauphin's gift: an enormous gilded chest? Beer barrel? Dirty paper bag held at arm's length in velvet gloves? Do they seem pleased or highly uncomfortable with the message and gift they are employed to deliver? After all, career diplomats tend to take their work seriously, and are not accustomed to delivering cheap jokes as official embassies. The Ambassador's question about whether Henry wants the answer diplomatically or straight-up may imply a certain discomfort with what he has to do, along the lines of 'please don't shoot the messenger'. When the Ambassador begins to deliver the Dauphin's message, we learn that Henry has already sent to claim 'certain dukedoms' (l. 247) in France as his ancestral right – perhaps Henry's advisors smile amongst themselves, knowing full well that the claim has already gone far beyond this. Once the extent of the Dauphin's scorn becomes clear, Henry and the English have several options. Henry can remain expressionless, giving nothing away of how he will respond, or he can begin to get wound up, or even start to smile as he sees where this is going. His advisors may shake their heads and chuckle at the Dauphin's mistake, or they may build up the tension by slowly turning to see how Henry reacts to the provocative reference to his wild youth. The revelation of the gift itself can be made by the French with a flourish, or left to Exeter; the former action would be a fitting conclusion to a full performance of French scorn, while the latter might indicate further unease on the messengers' part with the diplomatic faux-pas they are made to deliver. An altogether scornful embassy would probably lower our estimation of the French in general, while a group of uncomfortable diplomats might raise our estimation of them and only lower that of the Dauphin.

**258–97**  The Ambassador's message ends with a full line, the discovery of the tennis balls is made over a shared line between Henry and Exeter, and Henry's response begins on a full line – this would seem to indicate that no pause is taken for English gasps or for Henry to slowly rise with a killing look before he begins to speak. What seems to be called for is a quick and effortless beginning to this speech, which is probably the most effective method of creating tension because then everyone on stage and in the audience is waiting for the other shoe to drop. Henry is verbally quite dexterous here, immediately turning the Dauphin's gift around into elaborate images and puns about tennis balls, the game of tennis, and warfare. It is likely, as the speech continues and the actor warms and gains momentum, that the full emotional force of Henry's threats will be reflected in the delivery. If the speech descends into rant, however, it can become uncomfortable for everyone who has to listen to it. If there is fury in the delivery, it must be cool and controlled for Henry's response to have maximum impact in raising his stature. A key to our response to Henry lies in how we hear his lines ascribing blame for what is to come squarely on the Dauphin (ll. 282–8). We may hear this as bravado, or as a wholly appropriate response to a cheap joke made in such a serious situation, or we may think of Henry's other transferral of responsibility earlier in the scene when he warned Canterbury about 'what your reverence shall incite us to' (l. 20). If we think of this earlier exchange, we may start to suspect that transferring responsibility for his actions is something of a character trait. If so, we may not hear piety but another evasion when Henry concludes his threat to the French with 'But this lies all within the will of God.'

**298 to the end** The French embassy could exit terrified, chastened, relieved not to be executed for their message, or unrepentant in their scorn and unable to take this boy-king's threats seriously. Exeter's half-line may simply indicate a pause to let the French get off stage. Henry's council may be in awe at the passion the Dauphin's scorn unleashed in their leader, or self-satisfied in the now very public commitment to the cause they had been championing. They may indicate that, in their eyes, Henry has passed this test of leadership, and crowd around him in support and unity of purpose. Henry must take the energy of the scene into the call for action and mass exit he leads. All the choices thus far will determine whether that energy (and exit) is youthful and exuberant – with 'feathers to our wings' speeding him on – or knowing and calculated – 'we have now no thought in us but France' with a quick wink to the relieved clergy.

# ACT II

## Act II, Chorus

When the Chorus reappears asserting that 'all the youth of England are on fire' and that 'honour's thought' is now uppermost in everyone's mind, such gallant word-painting may seem mildly ironic if the previous Act has been played with calculations and self-interest on display. This gallantry may even get a laugh, if it overlaps the clergy making their exit either with quick glances of relief or with outright high-fives and a victory dance. If Act I has come across as more politic than chivalric, then we might reasonably wonder if the Chorus's version of the story seems at least a bit out of synch with what Shakespeare chooses to stage. If we have the thought, it's a fleeting one, as the Chorus is now moving us forward through high expectations and into details of a low plot by the French to 'divert the English purposes'. We are told of a conspiracy involving English noblemen and French gold, and a plot to murder the king in Southampton. 'The scene is now transported' to Southampton where the conspiracy is to play out; to Southampton 'do we shift our scene' for a royal tale of betrayal.

### Act II, scene i

Except we don't. Instead, in walk some of the low-life characters from Henry's earlier life – and earlier plays – to enact other stories of betrayal. This talk of 'the youth of England' from the Chorus is followed by a scene involving characters who have been around the block a few times. Talk of 'winged heels' pushing eager Englishmen forward to engage the French is followed by a scene of rather reluctant Englishmen squabbling among themselves and going nowhere. Most prosaically, all this talk of Southampton is followed by a London scene, presumably in Eastcheap. If we thought at the beginning that the Chorus was going to be a help to us in making our way through this history, we may think again as the Chorus's descriptive path seems regularly to be diverging from what is actually being performed. Is there an 'official' story? Is there a 'real' story? Is there a purpose to this dislocating manoeuvre, or is it just bad dramaturgy, or an unfortunate leftover from a revised manuscript?

As a play unfolds moment by moment in performance, we respond to developments in the story, as well as the development and deepening of the main characters. But we also respond to structure – what happens when, and why. When a play unfolds smoothly, linearly, logically, the structure seems transparent, even though it must have been carefully organized and paced to achieve that seeming transparency. But when scenes seem to bump into one another rather than flow, when sequences appear to be juxtaposed rather than seamlessly joined, we will start to look for some extra meaning being conveyed through those structural choices. We might hold the question in the back of our minds as to why events are structured the way they are, even as we are introduced to the so-called 'comic characters' and all their potentially colourful quirks.

**1–23**  If Act I gave us those who make wars, Act II begins with those who actually fight them. The exchanged greeting implies that Nim and Bardolph enter separately to meet on stage. Their appearance may provide quite a contrast to the splendour of the English court and French embassy, both in dress and in physical health. Whether this contrast is humorous or pathetic depends on casting and staging choices. Perhaps the first test case comes in Nim's threat – is it mock or real? – to 'wink and hold out my iron' when he meets his rival Pistol. He says his sword is 'a simple one' but the staging possibilities here are many. Nim may be a small man with a huge weapon, or a fat man with a tiny one, with all phallic connotations encouraged. His sword may be rusty, ragged, even home-made, which would add a pathetic note to his character (and to the potential make-up of the English fighting force), or it could be ostentatious and deadly, thereby adding some comic irony to all Nim's ambivalence and nonchalance before Pistol enters. Nim himself may be itching for a fight, pacing and waving his sword, or revelling in false bravado only because his opponent is safely absent, or may be angling for sympathy by playing sulky, sullen and hurt. The Act II Chorus is at least accurate in that we move to a story of betrayal, but in this case it is more domestic than international.

From Act I to Act II we've switched from verse to prose – they look different on the page, but don't necessarily have to sound that much different in the theatre. In this case, however, we also have very different vocabulary and sentence construction, as well as specific repeated catchphrases for Nim. On stage this may translate into a regional accent, or into stereotypical 'rustic'– a slow, laconic drawl perhaps – or urban 'low-life' – quick, whiny, fidgety – delivery patterns. Certainly some comic vocal approach is appropriate for a character who professes 'I say little' and then proceeds rather to go on a bit.

**24–42** The entrance of Pistol and Quickly seems to bring matters to a head. Perhaps Pistol and his new wife enter in some lascivious newlyweds' embrace that is just too provocative for Nim's wounded pride. After Nim's apparent slight of calling Pistol 'host' and Pistol's insulting reply, we have a number of implied actions in the dialogue about drawing swords and sheathing them again. At the very least, some kind of comic repeated rhythm of drawing and sheathing weapons will go on throughout the scene. The action between Nim and Pistol may start in Folio's line 'Now by this hand' (28, see the note in the Oxford edition) – Pistol may simply raise his hand to swear his oath, or he may reach for his sword, or he may grab Nim by the throat in a quick escalation of their feud. As for who actually draws and when, staging can of course vary. Quickly's sudden outburst (ll. 34–5) may indicate that Nim has drawn against her husband and he – Pistol – may be hewn, or she could be egging on her husband to draw so that he – Nim – will be hewn to avoid these dire (if slightly mangled in her phrasing) consequences. Bardolph could be physically keeping the combatants apart, and he may even have drawn his own weapon when he cautions them to 'offer nothing here'. When Quickly pleads with Nim to 'put up your sword' they may all back down for a (short-lived) moment, or the brawl might just get sillier with Nim wrestling to get Quickly out of his way – 'Will you shog off?' – so that he might have his nemesis *solus*. Of course, Nim might instead tell his enemy to shog off and whisper to Quickly that he'd like to see her *solus*. Either way, a little Latin is enough to rekindle Pistol's ire.

**43–77** If we had any doubts about what kind of scene this was, Shakespeare seems to make things pretty clear in the next exchange. For Pistol, drawn or not, his 'cock is up / And flashing fire will follow'. For Nim, his weapon is a match, and will serve to 'prick [Pistol's] guts a little'. These bawdy innuendoes may be funny, for those who involuntarily snigger when they hear the words 'cock' and 'prick', but they do at least confirm the exact nature of this contest between men, and the phallic weaponry being bandied about on stage makes the visual point too. What these men really want to know is, who has the bigger penis.

Most editors take Pistol's 'Therefore ex-hale!' to be a specific call to draw again, and the Quarto has the stage direction 'They draw' at this point in its version of the scene. It also seems implicit that Bardolph will have his sword drawn for his peacemaker's threat (l. 61). Pistol's 'fury shall abate' invites an all-round sheathing of swords once again. On stage, if Bardolph is less physically imposing than Nim and Pistol, then the cowardice behind their bravado would become perfectly obvious. The next exchange could conceivable engender another drawing of weapons to hammer again at this joke, but in staging, as in economics, there is a law of diminishing returns.

**78–85**   If things have been getting a little ridiculous, the entrance of the Boy adds a sober note. He asks that Pistol and Quickly both 'come to my master' – this master is not named yet, but if we've come with any knowledge of the *Henry IV* plays, we'll know this is Falstaff. The comment about Bardolph's face being used as a warming pan can serve as an implied direction to the make-up department about Bardolph's florid complexion. Before she rushes off, probably with the boy in tow, Quickly says of their sick friend 'The King has killed his heart.' Again, if we know anything about the *Henry IV* plays, we know that those plays concluded with a betrayal of sorts, as the new King disowned his old companions. If we thought this was fun and games, Shakespeare has chosen to add another layer, and a deeper level of hurt, for these characters.

**86 to the end**   Bardolph may be influenced by the news of Falstaff's illness to encourage the others once more to put aside petty arguments. But there is more pettiness where that came from, and Nim and Pistol's swords are out again by 'push home' to force Bardolph again to threaten them both with his sword. Pistol offers, finally, to make amends for a monetary if not marital debt with 'Give me thy hand.' This could imply that the two men finally come

together on a handshake, however grudgingly, or it could afford Nim
one last opportunity to be sullen and refuse the gesture. When
Hostess Quickly rushes back in, we know that Falstaff's illness is serious, even if we don't necessarily grasp the full medical implications
of a 'burning quotidian tertiary'. If the symptoms are obscure, the
cause is so plain that even recent enemies can agree on it:

> NIM    The King hath run bad humours on the knight, that's the even of it.
> PISTOL  Nim, thou hast spoke the right.

As the scene has been mostly comic *shtick*, the mass exit to 'condole'
Falstaff is likely to be quite solemn by comparison.

If the other shoe, structurally speaking, hasn't dropped yet, we
may now at least be aware it is dangling in front of us. The opening
Chorus promised us martial exploits, and so far we've had political
machinations and a pissing contest – and perhaps two such contests,
if we see Pistol/Nim as more echo than foil of Henry/Dauphin. The
Act II Chorus promised a tale of betrayal *of* Henry, but the first scene
of the Act ends with pointed references to a betrayal *by* Henry of his
old friend Falstaff. As with any good play, this one is telling more
than one story. Those stories will be commenting on each other, and
eliciting complex, sometimes even contradictory responses.

## Act II, scene ii

**1–11**    Now we get to the conspiracy the Chorus promised us.
However, instead of opening with those who are plotting against the
King, the Folio brings in three members of the King's council, who
reveal that the conspiracy has already been discovered. The Act II
Chorus told *us* all about this treacherous plot, but now at the beginning of the scene in which it should be enacted we find out that
Henry and his commanders know all about it as well. The scene is not
going to be about discovering and averting the conspiracy to kill
Henry, but rather about how Henry will trap the conspirators. This
choice would seem to take the urgency out of the unfolding action,
and in fact Exeter gives the impression (especially if delivered with a
laconic confidence) that what we are about to watch has all been

worked out in advance: 'They shall be apprehended by and by.' It is not a struggle but a display of power that Shakespeare chooses to dramatize here.

**11 stage direction**    Just how Henry's game of catch-the-conspirators reads to us may be determined by the make-up of the next entrance. The first line of the scene – 'Fore God, his grace is bold to trust these traitors' – makes a lot of sense when the Folio calls for Henry to enter with Scrope, Cambridge and Grey. It is at the least a gutsy move for the King to enter accompanied only by the three men he knows are plotting to murder him, without any officers, soldiers or attendants who could help him if his foes should choose that moment to strike. Most editors, however, add some if not all of the army to this scene. If a great number of Henry's men are on stage for what follows, the King will seem safer, but more importantly the scene will make sense as a public spectacle warning any other potential traitors not even to think about it – this king knows all, he'll catch you, and when he catches you you'll get no mercy. With a big onstage audience from the beginning, Henry's display of power would probably come across as good military policy for keeping everyone else in line. If the original stage direction is adhered to, then Henry would certainly seem bold but the scene would also become more personal. If the on-stage audience is not enhanced – leaving only the three commanders who already know all about it – then the whole display to come will seem more for Henry's own benefit than for anyone else's.

**12–24**    If the king is thought to be 'bold', we also know the demeanour of the traitors when they enter. Westmorland's earlier comment, 'how smooth and even they do bear themselves', implies they will not enter nervous, sweaty and shifty but rather calm and confident, perhaps even quite chummy with the man they are going to betray. Some ironic comedy may be had if Henry is just as warm and chummy with them. It may even appear that Henry is laying it on a bit thick when he addresses the three as 'my lord . . . my kind lord . . . and you, my gentle knight'. The irony could immediately turn quite vicious if Henry has an arm around one of them when he asks them breezy questions about his powers' ability to '*cut* their passage through the force of France, / Doing the *execution*' (my italics) for which they've been assembled. The irony is further compounded when Henry confidently, perhaps even pointedly, speaks of carrying 'not a heart with us . . . that grows not in a fair consent with ours'. As the scene progresses, we'll be watching just how the on-stage audience-in-the-know reacts to the compounding of ironies, and we'll be looking for signs of exactly when it starts to register with the conspirators that they are the ones being led into a trap, rather than the other way around.

**25–59**  As Scrope, Cambridge and Grey in turn reassure Henry (lines 19, 28, 31–2), Henry may have trouble keeping a straight face in the onslaught of such brazen bad faith. But Henry continues to give them enough rope to hang themselves. When he turns from the conspirators suddenly to address Exeter, we may think that this is the signal, that the trap springs now. Instead, Henry leads his enemies further in. Each conspirator, once again in turn, chides Henry for his proposed lenience toward this drunken railer, and again it may be hard for Henry – and Exeter, Bedford and Westmorland – not to smile as they walk into the trap, take the bait and practically close the door behind them. As Henry comes to the point of the story (ll. 53–6), the irony is breathtaking, the application almost too obvious; perhaps it is here that one or more of the conspirators starts to show something of that sinking feeling, especially if Henry is so physically close as to be literally rubbing it in with an arm around a neck or a slow pat on the back.

The whole sequence could be performed in deadly earnest with a steady building of tension, and clearly this is too serious a business to have the others whooping and rolling on the ground in laughter at 'jokes' the conspirators don't yet get. But it's hard not to believe that what Henry's doing here is, to some extent, *playing*. Is there a point when watching the cat bat the mice around makes us impatient for the kill, or even begins to make us shift our sympathies? As the irony continues, might we begin to doubt the total reformation of that formerly wild gamester Canterbury spoke of and the Dauphin alluded to?

**60–75**   When Henry moves on to ask about the 'late commission-ers' who just turn out to be Cambridge, Scrope and Grey, we might catch the bad pun about the (soon-to-be) dead men standing around him. 'There is yours . . . there yours . . . this same is yours' imply that some kind of official papers or folders to go with this office are handed to each conspirator, from Henry or his commanders. If the conspirators' sinking feeling hasn't come yet, surely it must after a quick glance at the papers and hearing the unmistakable meaning (whether delivered coldly, sarcastically or lightly) behind Henry's 'and know I know your worthiness'. Henry's lines strongly imply the kinds of reactions the sprung trap gets (ll. 68–73). It is a bit tough for an actor to turn pale on cue, but other signals – dropping jaws, widening eyes, held breath – can complement the description Henry provides. Cambridge finishes Henry's half-line (ll. 73–4) so the reaction is swift, but there is a pause indicated by Grey and Scrope's shared half-line – 'To which we all appeal' – that Henry for his part does not complete. The pause isn't needed for Henry to think about what to do, not after such a lengthy and detailed set-up. Henry may fill the moment physically by shaking his head and laughing at the idea they could even think of asking for mercy; maybe he just needs a good breath before launching into his 65-line rebuke.

**76–141**   Some editors indicate that the traitors all kneel before Henry, and this gesture is perhaps implied when Cambridge offers to 'submit'. They could go down and stay down all through Henry's speech, but other options are available. When the possibility of mercy is quickly denied, perhaps one or more of them suddenly moves to strike, bringing about some scuffling or even violent fighting before they can be disarmed by Henry and his commanders (or attendants if it is a bigger scene). Perhaps like cowards they try to run away, only to find Henry's commanders already drawn (or, again, the rest of the army surrounding them). If the traitors weren't kneeling on their own accord before, they probably are forced to now, and perhaps Henry just goes down the line when he starts by addressing Cambridge, moves on to Grey, and then finally gets to the worst offender, Lord Scrope.

Henry's rebuke takes up a lot of stage time, so finding a dramatically

effective way through it is key. The actor must decide whether the
speech was part of Henry's original script for his morality play, or if
it represents a real outburst of private passion. If it comes off like a
sermon, especially a holier-than-thou one, we, the parishioners, may
go to sleep. If it's one long angry rant, we'll likewise tune out. The
actor will have to modulate the rhetorical control and emotional
explosiveness of the attack. If this is a large, public scene before the
whole army, then Henry may be taking his time to make quite a spectacle of these men, so that the lesson of their fall is crystal clear. It
certainly could be played very intimately. All Henry's 'thees' and
'thous' (and his switch from the distanced 'us' and 'our' to the
personal 'I', 'me' and 'my') indicate the majority of the speech is
directly given to Scrope. Henry could be in his face, even making
contact if not actually physically delivering the kicking Scrope
deserves. The more distant the spatial relations between accuser and
accused, the more Scrope becomes Exhibit A in Henry's arguments
against betrayal; the more intimate, the more Henry appears to take
the betrayal, trap and punishment very personally. Henry could be
teaching about obedience, or he could be learning that private friend-
ships are past.

**142–78**   If Henry has held on to the traitors, metaphorically if not
literally, for his speech, he ends by turning them over to be arrested.
Exeter addresses each in turn – this formal speech perhaps implies a
formal gesture to go with it, such as taking back the three 'commis-
sions' again, or stripping off medals, ribbons or some other mark of
military or aristocratic distinction. When the three men repent and
ask for pardon, they may still be in shock at their abrupt turn from
hunters to hunted; they could be scared and in tears, like little lost
boys who are only starting to comprehend the trouble they're in;
they could be truly contrite, even serene in accepting their fates; or
their words could be grudgingly given, after the excruciatingly
prolonged spectacle Henry has put them through. If Henry seems
really to enjoy the set-up and springing of his trap, and if Henry's very
long speech to Scrope becomes emotional and physical (or deeply
sarcastic) as it plays out, Henry's assertion that 'Touching our person
seek we no revenge' may seem a bit disingenuous.

**179 to the end**   The traitors can be removed from the stage in a number of ways. They might be escorted solemnly away. They could be handled roughly and turned over to some who make it clear that extra punishment is in store before death. They could even be rushed off to immediate execution – perhaps we see the nooses being prepared or hear the shots if it is a modern-dress production; perhaps it is even done in front of us. Henry's address to those who remain could be an attempt to restore momentum to his enterprise, and pick his men up again with a quick pep talk refocusing attention on the real cause to hand; it might also serve as a warning coda to the whole display, with his on-stage audience in respectful admiration if not awe at his power. The scene ends with a linguistic flourish in Henry's rousing couplet (ll. 189–90). Now it is time for the real martial action.

## Act II, scene iii

Except it isn't. Instead, Shakespeare stages the other structural book-end to the official scene of betrayal. If we didn't think about Henry and Falstaff while we were watching Henry and the three traitors, Shakespeare gives us another opportunity. While Henry is sending 'poor miserable wretches' (II.ii.175) to their deaths, Shakespeare is sending another miserable man and one of his greatest dramatic creations to 'Arthur's bosom' (II.iii.9). While Henry in Southampton calls for his expedition to unfold their banners of war and take to water, Shakespeare makes us, and the action of the play, linger on unfinished domestic business and dry land back in London. Why does Shakespeare choose to envelop the story of the conspirators with the story of Falstaff's demise and death? We might compare the two stories, and then consider what Henry has to give up as he moves from private individual to public figure. Or we might contrast the two, and find Henry's overwhelming rhetorical anguish and talk of tears – 'I will weep for thee' – a little less convincing when faced with another group who actually must 'clear [their] crystals' (l. 48) as they weep over a man whose heart really was 'killed' by someone he loved turning against him. Depending on how cynical our dispositions already are about politicians and public figures, we may find ourselves contemplating the distinctions between the staged and the real, and not necessarily to the king's advantage.

**1–8**   There is potential for a great physical contrast from scene ii to scene iii. Henry and his men may exit with energy and purpose – 'Then forth, dear countrymen' – only to be followed on stage by Falstaff's plodding, grieving and slightly lost friends. Pistol gives his companions a little pep talk (an echo of the one Henry just gave?), implying that none of them are 'blithe' or 'vaunting' or have their 'courage up' when they enter. His attempt is met with the Shakespearean equivalent of 'I wish I was dead' from Bardolph. If they are just setting off or already on the road, as Quickly's first line indicates, then they come to an immediate standstill. Perhaps Quickly is encouraging them on to meet up with the King's forces, and it is Pistol who plops himself down on the ground, refusing to go any further – making his pep talk as much for himself as anyone else.

**9–39**   There is definitely an enormous linguistic/rhetorical contrast between Act II, scenes ii and iii. Henry's 65-line speech was about personal betrayal, but it was filled with extended, abstract imagery about demons and hell and finished with a sermon-like flourish about another fall of man; he asked rhetorically of Lord Scrope 'O what shall I say to thee?' and it turns out to be quite a lot. Hostess Quickly's much shorter speech about Falstaff's demise is filled with specific, concrete physical images of Falstaff's last moments. It's as if the enormity of the loss can only be approached by this steady progression of small details. It is a very natural and accessible speech, which means its emotional impact is likely to be much more direct; the moment is deepened because there is really very little to say – a brief description, a couple of jokes, a shared memory.

**40 to the end**   We know that Quickly has tears in her eyes by the end of the scene (l. 48), whether for Falstaff's death or her husband's departure or both. When Pistol finally turns his attention towards France, his bloodthirstiness here (l. 50) will be tempered by how much of a bragging coward he was in the almost-fight of Act II, scene i. On the other hand, if we have been 'moved' by their grief over

Falstaff, we might now be reminded that while the Eastcheap gang may be simpler, that doesn't necessarily mean they're nice people. At the end of the scene, Pistol kisses his wife – 'My love, give me thy lips' – and asks his friends to do the same – 'Touch her soft mouth, and march.' Bardolph and the Boy might obey Pistol's command, but Nim apparently will not. This can be handled in a number of ways: with Nim getting close and then changing his mind at the last second; with Nim offering to shake hands instead; with Pistol and Bardolph overruling him and dragging him over; or even with Quickly grabbing him and forcing a kiss to get past his still-sulky attitude towards her. But whether the sequence ends on a comic or poignant note for us may depend on how we feel about watching men go off to war and leave family behind.

### Act II, scene iv

'Thus comes the English with full power upon us' – if we heard these words after Henry's rousing finish to Act II, scene ii, the action would seem uninterrupted and the sentiments expressed dramatically self-evident. But coming after, or even overlapping, the exit of the Eastcheap stragglers makes them a bit ironic and potentially even laughable. The structuring again calls attention to itself. If there is a laugh at the juxtaposition, does it come at the expense of the English or the French? Perhaps Shakespeare uses the irony to get us to underestimate the English so that later events and outcomes will seem all the more spectacular. Productions can further develop the juxtaposition with their visual choices for the French court, which could be bright and rich or even gaudy, foppish and ostentatious. We might respond by favouring the 'simple' Englishmen over the opulent French, especially if we have a tendency to root for the underdog. If we are inclined to take a larger view, we might instead be pondering once again the contrast between those who make wars and those who fight them.

**1–75** The basic action of this scene is identical to that of Act I, scene ii – a king and his closest counsellors have a few moments to confer about an impending conflict before receiving a foreign embassy. In performance, many comparisons, and more likely contrasts, can be played up between the two courts and how they conduct themselves. If there is some tension in the English court before everyone speaks with one seeming voice, the French court appears a little more overtly fractious. Our first sign of discord among the French might be a performance choice afforded by a peculiar sentence structure in the opening speech. When the French King proposes how he will answer Henry's impending arrival (ll. 4–6), the sequence of names makes the King's son of lower status than the others, or even worse an afterthought to the main players in this royal defence. On stage, if the Dauphin perceives himself being slighted or even left out, he may verbalize his discontent with a sigh or a groan, or throw his arms up in impatience and dismay, forcing his father to turn to him and add him to the list.

Shared verse lines see the Dauphin interrupting his father (l. 14), the Constable interrupting the Dauphin (l. 29), and the French King and the Dauphin interrupting each other (lines 48, 75, 115) over the course of the scene. In performance, a physicalized and/or verbalized discontent at the first interruption at line 14 can very quickly give us a strong impression of the Dauphin's impatience and lack of respect for the situation or for those around him. Of course, when the Constable then interrupts him, we can get an equally strong idea of the lack of respect the others have for the Dauphin, especially if Berri and Bourbon add physical gestures, smiles or knowing looks that show them to be of the Constable's mind. We may see this suggestion of in-fighting in the French court as weakness; we may see this petty dissension as nothing compared with the plot against Henry's life by his own men that was dramatized earlier; or we may see the French King's inability to do much more than join the squabbling as demeaning for all and a stark contrast to the way Henry showed who was absolute boss in Act I, scene ii.

**75–95** When the French Ambassador arrived in Act I, scene ii, Henry had already declared 'Now are we well resolved.' When Exeter, the English Ambassador, arrives in Act II, scene iv, it is in the middle of a line, where the Dauphin is still trying to persuade his father about military strategy. The French King's interruption of his son (l. 75) could be played as much to shut the Dauphin up as it is to greet the new arrival. For his part, Exeter might show his enjoyment of the moment, if he thinks he's walked into a French court more wrangling than regal. The way Exeter delivers his message may again be in sharp contrast to the way the French embassy was played earlier. The content is certainly different – where the French were delivering a joke, Exeter is delivering a threat. If the French are glib and haughty (or fractious and openly divided) then Exeter might choose to deliver his message with cool, ruthless, businesslike efficiency. Of course, as we listen we might feel that the English embassy demanding the French King immediately turn over his crown is just as, if not more, ridiculous and insulting than the Dauphin's tennis balls.

**96–115**     Exeter's request for the crown is followed by a half-line from the French King: 'Or else what follows?' Exeter doesn't finish the line. The pause before his response can be filled with a vicious smile, or even with a freezing stare of incredulity, as if to say 'Don't you understand we mean business here?' In explaining that 'if requiring fail, [Henry] will compel', Exeter develops a moral position we've heard already – as in Act I, scene ii, the argument is made that the country being invaded, and not the invaders, will be responsible for all the horrors of war (ll. 105–9). However this is delivered by the actor, our reaction to this line of reasoning may depend more on whether we think it is a threat to try to get the French to back down (or roll over) and prevent war, or if we feel it is the specious logic of an undeniable aggressor.

**115 to the end**     The French King's answer – that he will respond tomorrow – is interrupted by the Dauphin, impatient of what reply Henry had made to his embassy. Exeter's relayed contempt may elicit non-verbal responses from the other French commanders, who may rather agree with Henry's estimation and who may also make it clear that they were not in support of the Dauphin's poor joke. The Dauphin may be momentarily shaken, but is more likely elated at the opportunity to go one-on-one with his English counterpart. The scene has an interesting false ending. The Folio indicates a flourish after the French King reiterates, 'Tomorrow you shall know our mind at full.' Some editors add a direction that the King rises here, as if formally to dismiss the embassy with these words. If so, then Exeter is being particularly brazen by refusing to be dismissed and instead adding another threat, and a piece of information – Henry 'is footed in this land already' – that may catch the French off-guard. If so, this news might provoke a response of fear or at least stop them in their tracks if they were all preparing to leave with the King. If Exeter momentarily wrong-foots the French, then the King's new end-of-scene lines will come off much weaker than the more curt dismissal he intended earlier. If Exeter really wanted to be brazen, he might also turn to leave after he drops his (potential) bombshell, undercutting the King by making him respond to Exeter's exiting back, thus rendering the second 'Flourish' even more pathetic.

# ACT III

## Act III, Chorus

The French in Act II, scene iv, might be momentarily taken aback at Exeter's news that Henry has already landed. The Act III Chorus appears to have missed the news altogether. Again, if we thought the Chorus was to be our guide, it is starting to seem regularly unreliable, or at least not particularly tied in to the actual stage action. The Chorus here spends almost 20 lines painting a vivid picture of Henry's fleet departing from the English piers – even though Henry called for that departure over 200 lines ago and, as Exeter has just indicated, Henry is already in France. 'Our swift scene flies,' as the Chorus says, but it flies against the current of the action. In other words, the Chorus gives us scene painting and stirring rhetoric that has already been surpassed by staged events; the Chorus is telling a story that is not the same as the story being enacted. The Chorus also paints a picture of an England left 'guarded with grandsires, babies, and old women', even though a large portion of Act I, scene ii, was spent deciding to send only a quarter of the army to France and leave three-quarters to protect the homefront. But the Chorus ends with an image of the siege of Harfleur, and gunners firing cannons. This particular image is not just painted in words but enacted with special effects, as '*chambers go off*' in the Folio stage direction. If there was a divergence, then the Chorus and the action have come back together again in a most striking, theatrical way, as 'down goes all' before Henry's attack.

## Act III, scene i

**1–2** But when the scene proper begins, Henry and his men appear to be in retreat because all did not go down before them. Henry's call for his men to go 'once more unto the breach' indicates that they have not yet succeeded, and the addition to his command, 'Or close the wall up with our English dead', indicates this might well be a last-ditch attempt along the lines of 'victory or death'. However, the punctuation in the Folio could imply stage action even more striking in nature. Henry's first line (in all modern editions), in the Folio is printed as two lines:

> KING　Once more unto the breach,
> 　　Dear friends, once more.

If Henry's speech begins with two half-lines, it may indicate two pauses (to which I've added possible directions) where his soldiers do not obey his command, twice:

> HENRY　Once more unto the breach,
> (*Pause. Henry looks at his men, but they do not move. He is almost incredulous.*)
> 　　(*Pleading*) Dear friends, once more;
> (*Pause. Still the men do nothing. Henry relents, disgusted.*)
> 　　(*Bitterly*) Or close the wall up with our English dead.

If this is played as a moment of group reluctance, sarcastic rebuke and personal despair, then Henry will have that much more work to do with the speech in order to turn things around. That, and the action, once more seems to veer away from expectations set up by the Chorus.

**3–17**    If Henry has to ask twice, and there is no mass exit after he asks, then we can imagine his next lines not as the beginning of some metaphor but rather as direct description (ll. 3–4). In other words, what he sees before him is the modest, still and humble (or humiliated?) soldiers, who are not jumping to obey his command. What he *wants* to see, here in the 'blast of war', is men who will 'imitate the action of the tiger'. The goal of his speech becomes moving his men from the one to the other; the goal is to change the stage picture. We've already had a few lengthy speeches from Henry, amply demonstrating his rhetorical skills, but this is the first speech where the rhetoric requires action in response – action that has not been predetermined but that hangs in the balance, in the moment. Henry must persuade, and it's not just hearts and minds but bodies that he really needs right now. Henry calls for a physical transformation in his men, and his rhetorical strategy is to describe each element of it in detail: 'Stiffen the sinews . . . disguise fair nature with hard-favoured rage . . . lend the eye a terrible aspect . . . let the brow o'erwhelm it . . . set the teeth . . . stretch the nostril wide . . . hold hard the breath . . . bend up every spirit to his full height.' These can all be cues for the actors playing Henry's soldiers as to how their physical demeanour changes over the course of the speech. Henry's tactics might involve enacting these things himself, or even going from man to man, literally, to mould each one into proper shape. The question for the soldiers is whether they resist and resent such treatment or rapidly warm to it.

**17–30**    Whether it's working or not, Henry changes from describing external attributes, to internal ones necessary for the fight; in doing so, he also starts blurring class lines in his fighting force. Henry exhorts the nobles on stage with him to 'Be copy now to men of grosser blood' – this is no time for aristocrats to worry about getting their uniforms dirty. On the other hand, he tells the 'good yeomen' in his audience that, despite being 'mean and base' by birth, they still have a 'noble lustre' in their eyes, and they too will fight for their honour's sake and their country's. Henry's message of mixing classes may again be physically enacted, with Henry pushing, pulling, cajoling and strong-arming his men to create a single group where there may at first have been some 'natural' (i.e. class) divisions.

**31 to the end**   Whether one or both of his main tactics worked, Henry appears to be describing the positive results of his words – and accompanying physical actions – in creating a new stage picture (ll. 31–2). If Henry has persuaded, then the proof will be in the (transformed) bodies that leave the stage with him for the attack, signalled by '*Alarum, and chambers go off.*'

Although the actor playing Henry has many choices to make in how to deliver the lines, and the soldiers in how to react, the meaning and effect of Henry's great speech also depends on the nature of the space in which it is performed. His words are going to come across quite differently depending on whether they are delivered within the giant frame of a large proscenium-arch theatre with detailed pictorial design representing the siege and to a large on-stage crowd of extras, or out on a small, open thrust and as much to the theatre audience as to (very few) other actors. If the former is the case, then we are watching action unfold. If the latter is the case, then we may become part of that action. The opening Chorus said the company would 'on [our] imaginary forces work'. If the space is intimate, if Henry is not divided from but out amongst the audience, and if he can see, make contact and interact with us – in other words, if we imagine a space like Shakespeare's Globe where the play was probably initially performed, rather than a modern pictorial stage – then over the course of Henry's speech we may literally become his forces in rallying for another charge. This is not to say audience members would leap onto the stage and follow, but rather that what Henry does to inspire the other characters he might also do to inspire us, to rouse us if not to scaling walls then to approval, cheers and heightened excitement, as if we too are part of the team.

## Act III, scene ii

But the next scene begins with those Henry did not persuade – perhaps not surprisingly, the ever-lagging Eastcheap crew. At least we know they caught the ships to get there. Act III, scenes i to ii, has a potentially awkward physical transition. The stage direction at the start of scene i calls for Henry, some of the nobility by name, and '*scaling ladders*'. It is probably safe to assume that Henry doesn't have to do all the work himself, or need to spend so much time rallying a few of his commanders – as many men as are available must come in to form Henry's army and to bear those scaling ladders. The beginning of Act III, scene i, when the army is in retreat and unable to break through, could be a staggered or somewhat confused mass entrance. But the end of the scene, when Henry has worked them up for another charge, surely needs a better exit than everyone filing off in an orderly fashion, or worse getting jammed up in the doors or wings, or even worse getting caught up with the actors trying to get on stage for the next scene. This may be mainly an architectural issue about entrance and exit points, but decisions still have to be made. Perhaps the Eastcheap gang *does* try to come on against the tide, as it were, with Bardolph offering his encouragement (with the others joining) to the exiting troops as he and the others squeeze past them onto the stage – the awkward physical transition becomes the comical character point. A more efficient and still comedic choice might be to have Nim, Bardolph, Pistol and the Boy on stage from the beginning of scene i, swelling the numbers, then yelling and cheering to help cover the mass exit while ultimately declining to join it.

The way we respond to this will depend on some of the choices already made about the Eastcheap characters. If they have been played primarily as comic relief, then we will probably see them as comic cowards weaseling out of the fight. If we have been allowed or encouraged to take them seriously as well, then their response to Henry's rousing speech could add another legitimate voice and perspective on the action.

**1–26** Nim doesn't want to join because 'the knocks are too hot' and he doesn't have a 'case of lives' to offer up; perhaps his reluctance is only natural in the face of becoming cannon fodder in a foolhardy frontal assault. Pistol's response – that 'Knocks come and go, God's vassals drop and die' – could then seem philosophical, or bitter, or resigned, but at least worthy of our consideration as the role in which lesser mortals see themselves during the king's pursuit of honour. So too might the Boy's desire to be 'in an alehouse in London' come across as understandable regret rather than comic cowardice. When Fluellen enters and, according to the Quarto, '*beats them in*', we may see this as just a necessary prevention of insubordination during the battle, or even as a bit of broad comedy if the men scatter, trying to avoid Fluellen like little boys playing tag. But if this beating is particularly severe – Pistol asks four times for Fluellen to abate his rage, which could indicate an overly prolonged thrashing – then our comedic satisfaction at these slackers' comeuppance may dissolve into other questions about class structure and the treatment of the troops.

**27 to the end**     The Boy is left on stage for his long speech, but there is some uncertainty as to whether Fluellen stays or goes off after the others. If Fluellen leaves, then we get a bitter soliloquy from the Boy that undercuts any romantic notions (if we had them) about the Eastcheap crew, as well as any confidence in Henry's rhetorical construction (if we bought into it) of the noble soldier, in Act III, scene i. If Fluellen stays, we may get that plus another layer of visual irony. Some editors add a stage direction calling for Fluellen's exit on the grounds that if he stayed on stage he would appear to be himself getting out of precisely what he had just physically forced the others to do. Of course, in performance that could become precisely the point, if the desire was to show some hypocrisy and reluctance further up the chain of command. In that case, Fluellen, after such physical exertions (if only against his own men), could kick back, take a rest, even pull out a book to give a visual clue about his pedantry to come regarding the disciplines of the war.

**Act III, scene iii**

**1–80**     When Gower catches up with him, Fluellen – who has just driven complaining, reluctant men to the front – is now himself quick to complain about the way the siege is unfolding, and reluctant to 'come presently to the mines' as ordered by his superior, the Duke of Gloucester. When Gower the Englishman and Fluellen the Welshman are joined by Jamy the Scotsman and MacMorris the Irishman for a good round of bickering (even though they all seem to agree things are not going well), perhaps we just end up with a broad comedy of competing (broad) accents. However, we may again

wonder about the way Shakespeare structures things. The reluctant
Eastcheap crew is on stage for less than 20 lines in Act III, scene ii
before they get beaten up to the line. The multinational forces of
scene iii complain and argue amongst themselves for about 80 lines
until they realize the battle has stopped. MacMorris may rage that 'It
is no time to discourse' but discourse they do, and once again the
English soldiers are fighting amongst themselves. What we don't see
is the English army fighting any French.

**81–9** The multinational discussion on the disciplines of war that
turns into ethnic infighting is halted by the town of Harfleur sounding a parley – an invitation to talk between the two warring parties
– and by a mass entrance of '*King Henry and all his train before the gates*'.
Unlike his men, Henry wants no further discourse than this: 'This is
the latest [i.e. last] parle we will admit.' Henry has not come to negotiate but to offer an ultimatum (ll. 83–5). Henry's strong words come
at an interesting moment in the battle as Shakespeare chooses to
dramatize it. To recap Shakespeare's choices: at the beginning of the
Act, Henry is calling his men not *to* the front but *back to* the front
after a retreat, after one or more unsuccessful attempts to break
through the breach; Henry's long speech is designed to remake
reluctant men back into a unified fighting force. Then we get some
unwilling participants complaining and ducking out of the fight,
who require not rhetoric but a prolonged beating to move them
into the action. Then we get commanders who also complain about
the course of the battle before they too begin fighting amongst
themselves. We hear from Fluellen that the English effort to blow up
the town's fortifications with mines is in disarray and more likely to
'plow up all', English included. MacMorris then emphatically
confirms, 'O 'tish ill done, 'tish ill done, by my hand 'tish ill done,'
and himself complains 'we talk and, be Chrish, do nothing, 'tis
shame for us all'. The only staged violence in Shakespeare's version
of the battle for Harfleur is Fluellen beating his own men and, possibly, MacMorris threatening to cut off Fluellen's head (l. 73) for a
perceived slight, but being held back by Jamy and Gower. Before
Henry returns to the stage to demand total, unconditional surrender, the English effort at Harfleur really appears not to be going so

well. In terms of what Shakespeare dramatizes, Henry isn't in much of a position to make that demand.

We might account for this discrepancy by deciding that professional soldiers are by nature also professional complainers, no matter what the state of a battle. Productions can add much sound and fury around and underneath the scenes Shakespeare provides, to give a sense of more going on than what the Eastcheap and multinational folks are involved in. We could perhaps think Henry is bluffing when he calls for surrender; this option may make psychological and even tactical sense, but if the actor in any way lets on that he's bluffing, the bluff isn't going to work, so it's not really a *playable* option on stage and in the moment. Perhaps Shakespeare is just showing us, once again, that there is a difference between rhetoric and action.

**90–123**     If so, the remainder of Henry's speech will test that distinction in a particularly profound way. If Harfleur does not open its gates to the English, then Henry says the English will close the 'gates of mercy' to the citizens of Harfleur. No mercy means not just defeat but rape, infanticide, atrocity; Henry's men will go not just for the kill but for overkill. Since the self-appointed resident expert, Fluellen, says nothing here, we'll have to decide for ourselves if these threats are in accordance with the disciplines of war. If strong rhetoric has been successful in moving his own men to do what Henry wanted (and especially if that was the last and only successful action we saw in the Harfleur campaign), then perhaps it will work to move the French to do what he wants as well. But Henry has to say it like he means it – whether delivering the threats full-bloodedly and in full voice, or with calm, cool, fearful certainty – and he must remake his soldiers once again from the noble 'greyhounds in the slips', earlier, into the hounds of hell, here. If his men responded physically to Henry's rhetorical make-over earlier, it would be interesting to see if they do so here, and how. If this is a real threat and no bluff, then perhaps Henry is just stripping away the fine rhetoric to reveal what soldiers and war are really all about. Henry's dog-soldiers could show their awe at the rhetorical violence he unleashes, or they could quickly get with the new programme and become the 'rough and hard of heart . . . bloody-hunting slaughtermen' Henry threatens literally to unleash, or they could non-verbally signal discomfort with or even some resistance to this new, hardly noble role.

If we, the audience, were (willingly) drafted into Henry's army in Act III, scene i, then we might find ourselves implicated in Henry's rhetoric now as well. Is this a comfortable position for *us* to be in, and just how bloodthirsty are *we*, as willing participants in the drama? Are we supportive of Henry's argument, which blames the victim here (lines 99, 123), and ready to see carried out the action Henry describes? If we have already decided we like Henry, if we are on his side, then we might see his strong words in a very positive light – namely, that strong words may prevent actual violence. If the French can be persuaded rather than slaughtered, then Henry's vile words serve as a prevention of vile deeds, and the rhetoric of violence may actually save lives.

**124 to the end**    The theatrical 'fact' is that Harfleur capitulates after this speech, and there is no scene (or report) of Henry's threats being carried out. Harfleur chooses mercy, and that is what Henry instructs Exeter to dispense: 'Use mercy to them all.' But we may still wish to ask whether Henry can make the extended, detailed image of sickening violence and immediately take it back once it works, without being affected or tainted in the process. Whether a bluff or a possibility not acted upon, Henry's words are likely to have some effect on us in our response to Henry's character, and on our willing complicity in the unfolding action. On stage, words can take on much of the force of reality. Words are often what we have to go on, and in this speech their force cannot be undercut or softened with contradictory physical action as they are being delivered – the action dictates that they need to work. If Henry is capable of these words, then at the least we must consider whether Henry and his army are capable of these actions. After the speech, Henry's lines may indicate that he was bluffing or at least overplaying his hand. He talks of 'sickness growing upon our soldiers' and immediately decides to 'retire [i.e. retreat] to Calais' – those lines make sense both with and of the earlier scenes of English discord and disarray. He might physically relax and signal his relief. So, probably, will his men. But in the moment of delivery, especially when nothing of the actual battle between French and

English for Harfleur is called for, dramatized or visualized in the
script, these images of atrocity are what we have, even if they are ultimately 'only' left ringing in our ears.

## Act III, scene iv

If Shakespeare had wanted to keep the action moving, he would have
gone from the English victory over Harfleur in Act III, scene iii,
directly to the French regrouping and responding to that defeat in Act
III, scene v. Instead, we get a scene with Princess Catherine and her
waiting-woman. Again, if a scene doesn't directly advance the action,
then we have to look for other reasons why it is there, especially if its
content seems a notable juxtaposition with what comes before and
after. Perhaps it is meant to provide a tonal shift, from the darkness,
violence and high stakes of warfare to a pretty, charming scene with
female characters and lovely frocks. Perhaps we are meant to be reas-
sured, after the talk of shrill-shrieking daughters being raped, by
seeing the daughter of the French King safe, unharmed and at play.
The scene might serve as a signal that this is where our story is going,
rather than the grim direction the Harfleur speech might have
momentarily indicated. Perhaps the scene is not meant as a juxtaposition, a tonal shift, or a reassurance. Perhaps it is a political scene, and
Shakespeare's continuation of Henry's warfare by other means. The
charming language lesson that plays out here is of Catherine's body
being 'Englished' – which is precisely what will happen if Henry's
imperial enterprise is successful. The actors can play the scene lightly,
joyfully, as if the lesson is fun, exotic or romantic; the scene can be
filled with laughter, on stage and in the audience. On the other hand,
the actors could play the scene more seriously, with some underlying
tension or anxiety in their physicality and voices; the actors could play
the scene with a keen political awareness that, if Henry and his army
are winning, then they'd better start learning English. Ending the scene
with translation jokes about 'fuck' and 'cunt' may keep us much closer
to the threats of rape from the previous scene than we at first might
have expected. Whether we see a fun and frivolous or a serious and
discerning Catherine here will make a big difference to our percep-
tions of her (and by extension of Henry) at the end of the play.

## Act III, scene v

**1–4**   When the Governor of Harfleur gave up the town to Henry, he said that the Dauphin's 'powers', on which he had been relying, hadn't materialized because they were not ready yet. Act III, scene v, begins with the self-recriminations, bitterness and urgency of the French commanders who displayed such a lack of urgency before. This could be immediately indicated in the mass entrance to start the scene, with a potential multitude of French Lords literally chasing the King on, hounding him to take strong action. After his first line, the French King doesn't speak again for another 35 lines – he may be in shock, or may be weighing his options while the others chatter on.

**5–35**   All the subsequent talk of stock and grafting and bastards extends Henry's threats of rape, and the Englishing of Catherine's body parts, into a particularly inglorious peril to French manhood (ll. 28–31) – unless, of course, we have already decided that the Dauphin is a comic character, in which case his image and the dismay of all the French may just be meant for a jingoistic laugh, especially if earlier production choices have made the French out to be effete, ineffectual and deserving of a little ridicule in comparison with the hardy and resourceful (and more 'manly'?) English.

**36–55**   When the French King finally rouses himself, his speech is both noble and powerful. The great list of multi-syllabic French names can be forceful, dignified and aurally magnificent when spoken aloud. The command to 'Bar Harry England' can galvanize the bickering French Lords from Act II, scene iv, but the caveat 'you have power enough' can be a subtle or pointed dig at the Dauphin who let Harfleur down, and at anyone else who underestimated Henry to allow him to progress as far as he has.

**55 to the end**   The scene ends with a grand call to action but also with a potentially comic domestic moment. The French Lords are sent off to secure Henry's fall, but the Dauphin is instructed to stay with Daddy. The Constable already has a potentially haughty line when he assumes Henry will fold as soon as he sees the real French army, but if he and the others also snigger and smile at the Dauphin's expense while leaving – or if the Dauphin has something of a tantrum – then we may once again be left with an impression of a French side arrogant, petty and divided against itself, and a hint that the French perhaps don't quite have their act together yet.

## Act III, scene vi

**1–18**  When Gower and Fluellen meet to discuss the English progress in their marches, the story of the battle for a bridge is perhaps not the most critical moment in the English campaign, but it is a crucial moment in the development of several of our key characters. Fluellen's news that 'gallant service' was done at the bridge by 'as valiant a man as Mark Antony' and that this man is none other than Pistol, demands some response. If Pistol and all the Eastcheap gang have been portrayed as comic relief or a collection of braggart cowards and assorted low-life, and Fluellen has been portrayed as a pompous windbag with his nose in a history book and no sense of actual warfare, then this revelation might be a comically timed surprise asking for laughter at both Pistol's and Fluellen's expense. But a production could just give us this information straight, forcing us to take it at face value and qualify (or complicate) our responses to Pistol accordingly – Fluellen specifically says he 'did see him' perform heroically, and so a braggart and shirker may also be capable of acquitting himself with distinction in the field.

**19–61**  Shakespeare moves directly into a more complicated situation – Bardolph's arrest and imminent execution for stealing. When Pistol arrives, he may be trying valiantly to save the life of a friend, or he may just be trying to weasel around the rules. Fluellen may be an insensitive windbag in going on about painted Fortune, or he may be trying, kindly, to find some way to let Pistol know that such matters are simply out of their hands. Pistol's continued desperate efforts on Bardolph's behalf may be heartbreaking and painful to watch, an emotional outpouring from a man used to talking tough. On the other hand, the speech could end with an attempted bribe – 'Speak, captain, for his life, and I will thee requite' – which might seem sleazy instead, and a dishonour to Fluellen. Perhaps it's the desperate emotions that lead to the sleazy bribe. At any rate, both men harden into their 'roles' – Pistol as a foul-mouthed bully and Fluellen as an inflexible rule-monger. Pistol can exit in an ugly fury at not getting his way, or in tears of despair at losing his last, best chance to save a friend.

**62–89**    The exchange between Gower and Fluellen that follows – a fairly thorough demolishing of Pistol's character – may seem fitting given what we already know, or it might seem gratuitous kicking of the man when he's down. It may also seem curious that Pistol received praise for, presumably, killing Frenchmen at the bridge, but ridicule for trying to save the life of an Englishman. However, Fluellen may be deflated here too, as he now seems to backtrack – to save face? – by talking of Pistol's 'prave words at the pridge' rather than brave actions.

**90–114**    Henry's entrance with '*his poor soldiers*' according to the Folio direction seems to indicate that the army's fortunes have been in steady decline since the victory at Harfleur, and this may be reflected on stage in the grimy dress, exhausted looks and dog-tired bodies of the men who make this less-than-energetic mass entrance. But whatever state they are in from the marches, perhaps the greatest test of strength for Henry comes when Fluellen tells him of Bardolph's impending demise. Fluellen's question – 'if your majesty know the man' – and the detailed physical description may be innocent enough on his part, but it is surely most pointed on Shakespeare's. Of course Henry knows the man, and if his soldiers aren't necessarily watching to see if their leader blinks here (though they could be, especially if Pistol is back on stage again), we in the audience certainly are. The death of one former friend in Act II was removed from Henry's presence, but the death of this friend may take place directly off stage or even be brought on stage for the king to authorize – after all, Bardolph's theft is being made an example of, so that example may be best made right in front of all the troops whose behaviour it is meant to guide. Henry's response to Bardolph's plight – 'We would have all such offenders so cut off' – may be cold, distant, and another shedding of his humanity, or it may be an excruciating moment for a leader who must uphold the rules no matter what his personal stake in the matter. Does Henry pause before he makes this pronouncement? Does he falter at all as he is making it? Or does he speak immediately, strongly, and with moral certainty? If Pistol has come back on stage to hear and see this, is he furious, stunned, or wordlessly pleading with his former friend? If Henry is unmoved and unhesitating in his public capacity here, he may show the deeper personal cost of this decision sometime later.

**115–35**   Montjoy's entrance offers at least two striking visual possibilities. First, his arrival may come just as the English are executing one of their own men – Montjoy might smile and register this event as a good thing, with the English apparently turning on themselves, or find it deeply unnerving, as an example either of strict discipline or of ruthless brutality. Of course, Henry can play the moment with a wince at the supremely bad timing, or poker-faced as though death, even and especially of his own men, is not something to faze him in the slightest. Secondly, Montjoy's arrival in some spotless, opulent 'habit' whereby he is known would be an extraordinary contrast to the 'poor soldiers' littered about the stage. When Montjoy delivers the French King's threats, the soldiers hearing him may react as if this is adding insult to injury. The already downtrodden men could fall further into fear and despair, or they could react to these words of French might with derision and disregard, and the end of the speech might find them standing a bit taller in defiance.

**136–66**   Henry's speech starts like an admission of weakness, but by the end becomes a potent counter-threat. Henry can play the speech like a bait-and-switch, with a physical and vocal delivery that is slow, strained and vulnerable to start – 'tell thy king I do not seek him now . . . My people with sickness are much enfeebled' – but that moves through a sly joke about the bragging he must repent, through to a 'rediscovery' of the voice (and promise of violence) we last heard outside the gates of Harfleur (ll. 159–61). Henry finishes with a half-line – 'So tell your master' – and a pause might indicate Montjoy is indeed taken aback at the ferocity of this response, and the clever rhetorical reversal. But the exact opposite is also possible. The lines could indicate that Henry repeats himself, stops and starts, changes direction and offers multiple commands to Montjoy through the speech, like he is scrambling and struggling and slowly losing it in front of the enemy – in which case the pause at the end is because the speech just dies out. Psychologically, the ferocity or the confusion of Henry's response here might be the delayed effects of the emotions (anger, frustration, loss?) he had to suppress earlier when ordering Bardolph's execution.

**167 to the end**   When Montjoy exits, Gloucester's line may reflect a fear they all feel, regardless of the display they may have put on when Montjoy was present. Henry's response can be said with resignation, or with new-found strength of purpose. The physicality of the mass exit of Henry and his soldiers can be used to show further decline in spirits, or something like a second wind and new resolve.

## Act III, scene vii

Act III, scene vi, is packed with incident, and can be an emotional rollercoaster; by contrast, Act III, scene vii, appears to be a static scene about waiting. Of course, a lot can still be revealed in exactly *how* people wait. In this case, the French seem by turns lazy, boastful, arrogant, catty and guilty of some hyperbole in singing the praises of a soldier's equine companion. This can be played for laughs as characteristic foppishness, disunity and frivolity, if that is the approach a production has been taking with the French thus far. But the scene could also be played, and perhaps be more effective dramatically, with the kind of strained silences, desperate bravado and quick irritability that are the result of heightened tensions before battle, if the French are being given a little more credit. The more ridiculous the French appear, the less formidable opponents for the English they become. This could be a strategy in performance, if the decision is to make the action of the play about French fools getting their comeuppance at the hands of the plucky English. But we can, and probably should, still take the 'other' side seriously – after all, it's not as though we haven't seen plenty of disunity and peevishness played out amongst the English. The scene can be played languorously, with the only energy the bored French expend coming in out-boasting or sniping at each other – however, a scene of bored people just being bored can make for deadly boring theatre. On the other hand, each character can be played as prickly and on edge, with the result being a steady ratcheting up of tension in the scene, and an understanding on our part that we are watching men who will die tomorrow.

# ACT IV

## Act IV, Chorus

This speech contains some of the most visceral language and intense and evocative imagery in the play; here the Chorus's scene painting is likely to be overwhelmingly effective in conjuring up time and place for us. From the 'hum of either army' to the 'secret whispers' of the watches, from the horses' neighs 'Piercing the night's dull air' to the 'busy hammers closing rivets up', we get a particularly vivid and detailed soundscape. From the 'paly flames' of the campfires to the 'umbered faces' of the soldiers who sit by them, from the 'overlusty French' who 'play at dice' for their coming conquests to the 'lank lean cheeks and war-worn coats' of the English, who reflect the moonlight like 'So many horrid ghosts', we have strong visuals from which to imagine the appearance of both sides. Productions may choose to create such a soundscape and stage such visuals, either during the Chorus's speech or in the next scene. But the strongest and most important image the Chorus offers is in the contrast between this 'foul womb of night' and the man who walks through it 'like the sun' giving 'comfort' to and 'Thawing cold fear' of everyone he meets. The 'cripple tardy-gaited night' limps along like some 'foul and ugly witch' but Henry moves among his men 'with a modest smile' and gives 'no note' of fear but rather 'freshly looks . . . With cheerful semblance and sweet majesty'. According to the Chorus, this 'little touch of Harry in the night' does more to warm his men than the fires they huddle around. The image of Henry moving amongst his soldiers is powerful enough just in the telling, but it also feels like an implied stage direction and acting note for Henry's conduct to come, and a guide to the tenor of the soldiers' reactions whenever they encounter him.

## Act IV, scene i

**1–35**   The scene begins with Henry counselling his brothers that great danger must be faced with even greater courage, and with a warm and joking exchange with Erpingham. Henry's line that their 'bad neighbour makes us early stirrers' may imply that there is indeed an ongoing soundscape of French noise, partying, and general carrying on that keeps the English awake and on edge. But this seeming replication of what the Chorus has just described lasts only a few lines before Henry borrows Erpingham's cloak to disguise himself and begs leave of their company desiring solitude instead (ll. 32–3). The disguise would seem to ensure that any 'touch of Harry in the night' will now not be known as such; and what exactly is it that Henry needs to debate? Does he need the solitude because he's exhausted by the strain of being modest and cheerful and 'like the sun' in public for his men? Is this where the episode of Bardolph's execution (among other things) catches up with him – will he be debating what he's given up for this foreign campaign, given up to be king? Perhaps we will see the interior Henry, see the inner workings of the great leader – after all, we have had many public speeches but no soliloquies from our main character yet. Henry's physical attitude when his men leave might signal what is to come – is he calm or evasive, friendly or tense? The commander can't show fear to his men, but he might be showing the strain of not showing that fear. The Folio marks Erpingham and the others' exit before Henry says 'God-a-mercy, old heart, thou speak'st cheerfully' – if Henry, now alone, strongly emphasizes 'thou' he could indicate that his own cheerfulness has been forced, and that his mood in reality is much darker.

**36–64**   Before Henry has a chance to soliloquize, he is subject to some chance encounters. He said he wanted to be alone, which would seem to imply that each encounter is unlooked-for on Henry's part, and Henry can certainly signal that, on stage, with a physicality indicating he is 'caught' each time. It may seem prosaic, but it is crucial to decide just how thorough a disguise Erpingham's cloak actually is for Henry – a huge, dark, hooded cloak may make Henry seem ghostly, even threatening in appearance, his 'sun' quite eclipsed, while a minimal concealing might be comic, or perhaps bitterly ironic as the scene moves on.

At any rate, Pistol does not seem to recognize him when they cross paths. Henry has said he wants to be alone, but the script doesn't necessarily dictate what Pistol is doing here. He may be acting as a watchman or sentry, guarding the camp and interrogating any passer-by – even though, bizarrely, he does this in French. At the other end of the performance spectrum in staging Pistol's character, perhaps Henry stumbles upon him in the act of picking some sleeping soldier's pockets, in which case his low-life stature is visually confirmed and his bravado merely an attempt to cover his tracks. What is most interesting, however, is this sudden outpouring of affection for Henry (ll. 45–9), spoken as it is just to some stranger, and not so long after Bardolph's execution. Even more interesting is that after this outburst, Pistol and the stranger-who-is-actually-Henry immediately get into an argument, one that is, if not provoked, at least egged on by Henry, even if it ends with an obscene gesture from Pistol to go with 'fico for thee'. This may be funny – or it may be a pointed measure of how far Henry has moved, cloak or not, from the man Pistol once loved.

But the playing could make clear that Henry and Pistol do instantly recognize each other. When Henry introduces himself as 'a friend', Pistol's questions (ll. 38–9) might not be necessitated by the dark so much as by Henry's change in character – if Pistol recognizes him physically, he may wish to know if Henry is now friend only to officers, or still to commoners. If Henry is then evasive (l. 40) Pistol's outburst could be an attempt to remind Henry of who he was and what he meant to his old friends. But Henry continues his evasions, sticks to his 'disguise' and makes his choice – if, when asking about Fluellen, Pistol emphasizes 'art thou his friend?' then the choice is clear, and Henry chooses Fluellen. The encounter could be played as another plea, betrayal, and stripping away – there is no old Henry, no 'lovely bully' and no old friends – and thus become a heartbreaking moment where two men reluctantly agree not to know each other.

**65–81**   The encounter with Pistol may be unwanted, or difficult, or even quite unpleasant. But when Gower and Fluellen enter, they do not encounter Henry at all. Perhaps Henry hears them coming – after all, that's what Fluellen goes on to chastise Gower about – and steps aside, ducks into a shadow, or pretends to be either occupied or asleep. Perhaps Gower and Fluellen walk right past Henry and just ignore him. The difference is significant: in the first possibility, Henry is in control and active in picking his encounters, choosing to engage or avoid; in the second, the King simply becomes less significant on stage when in his disguise, and that once vividly described little touch of Harry now visually/physically fades even further into the night.

For Gower and Fluellen, a few jokes are possible in their exchange. One is that Gower could follow Fluellen on and shout after him, sparking Fluellen's lengthy, historically footnoted request for him to be quiet. The other is that Gower's two words, even if softly spoken, are two too many for the effusive Fluellen to bear, and simply must be countered by a flood of verbiage to compensate. Gower's protest that 'the enemy is loud. You hear him all night' might again imply that the sounds from the French camp are underlying the scene. A further aural joke might be for Fluellen to have to speak louder himself to be heard over some of the outbursts coming from the French tents, or for Fluellen to get so worked up in countering Gower that he starts to yell, realizes it, checks himself, and drops back down to a whisper at the end. Gower and Fluellen may then leave together, or one last joke could come with Fluellen finishing his lecture and storming off, leaving poor Gower to realize he never got to say whatever it was he had to say to Fluellen in the first place and so forcing him to chase after Fluellen once again.

**82–9**   Henry is left alone, but after only two lines – delivered to us after the exiting Fluellen, like his earlier line after the exiting Erpingham – Henry's solitude is once again interrupted with the arrival of John Bates, Alexander Court and Michael Williams. Unlike the others Henry has encountered, we don't know these men. We may have seen them as members of Henry's on-stage army in earlier scenes, but we have no expectations of who they are or what they are like. For Shakespeare to introduce three new characters at this stage of the play – over two-thirds of the way through the action – implies some extra significance for this encounter. The initial attitude of these three soldiers (ll. 88–9) immediately takes us back to the Chorus's image of the 'poor condemned English', those ordinary soldiers who are spending their night 'ruminat[ing] the morning's danger', and they might seem to be just the kind of 'wretch[es], pining and pale' who could use the comfort that the Chorus said Henry delivers. Williams either sees or hears Henry – 'Who goes there?' – but what occasions this interrogation is important. Perhaps Henry is retreating into the darkness and trips over something, making a noise that the jumpy soldiers immediately challenge. Perhaps, hidden in the folds of Erpingham's oversize cloak, Henry cuts such an obviously bizarre figure that only the self-absorbed Fluellen could possibly miss him. Perhaps Henry steps forward to bestow that promised 'largess universal' upon his fearful men, which would be ironic if all three men instead instantly draw their weapons.

**90–6**   If we expect at least this encounter to run something like what the Chorus so optimistically described earlier, then Henry's initial stance hints we are about to be a third time disappointed. Henry chooses not only to maintain his anonymity but also to do less than comfort the soldiers by declaring, falsely, that Erpingham too believes they are all doomed. If we thought Henry was going to step forward to cheer them up, then this seems a strange way to begin doing it. Henry, in his anonymity, may just want to be like his common soldiers, and so adopts their attitude with a laugh and a knowing look. Perhaps, as commander of this army, he quietly throws out some bait to find out just how low morale really is – he may secretly fear his men were just humouring him earlier, and now see an opportunity to get the unvarnished truth. He may just want to blow off some steam under the cover of his disguise, by playing a trick or stirring up trouble like he used to do in his good old, bad days. Perhaps, rather manipulatively, he is even setting himself a challenge to see how low men can be and still have his presence and/or rhetoric pick them up again. The actor may throw the line out firmly, or tentatively, but because we didn't get any soliloquy from him at first, we can't be entirely sure of Henry's intentions here – we can only go by the action as it unfolds.

**97–109**   Bates's response to the report of Erpingham's pessimism may imply that these soldiers are taken aback – it's okay for the grunts to have doubts, but for a commander to have them, and admit to them, doesn't bode well for anyone, especially those who will be on the front lines. If Bates responds here and in his later lines with an ironic laugh and gallows humour, the soldiers might be sharing the bitter joke that they are all screwed in the morning. But Henry turns things into an extended disputation on the King being just like anyone else. Does Henry wish he were 'but a man' again, instead of the public figure he finds himself subsumed in – is this what he and his bosom wanted to debate? Or have his anonymous encounters just now started to shake his confidence and make him think that he isn't that glowing sun the Chorus advertised, once the costume for that role is no longer apparent? Whatever this means for the disguised Henry's psyche, the soldiers might laugh at this special pleading, or begin indicating some discomfort and distress at this notion that the King is just a man – they might not *want* the King to be just a man, especially not one who is afraid. They might need him to be much more than that if they have any hope of getting through the next day. If this is expressed physically through uneasy shifting and anxious glances, then perhaps Henry picks up on it – 'Yet, in reason . . .' – to reverse or qualify himself in saying that no one, king included, should show any fear.

**110–28**   But it's too late. Bates now imagines the King wishing he were back in England, forcing Henry to contradict him with an assurance that the King is happy where he is. Bates's (quite possibly bitter) response to this forces Henry to go even further in claiming that the notion of dying here with the King should give them all content (is this the comfort the Chorus spoke of?) since 'his cause [is] just and his quarrel honourable'. Williams doesn't buy this, and if Bates contends that obedience means it doesn't matter anyway, Williams won't let it go and pushes on to articulate the deepest misgivings we've heard yet about the whole campaign. It is possible that we are witnessing, in this scene, the first time in the play that Henry isn't leading the conversation, that Henry's words do not make things better but in fact make them worse, and that other voices offer just as compelling if not a more compelling view of reality than the title character.

**129–40** Williams's vision of the fate of soldiers in battle, of 'legs and arms and heads chopped off' and of wives and children left behind and destitute as a result of the men's death, is a kind of anti-Chorus, and about as diametrically opposed in content to that official cheerleading as we might imagine. The playing style can also be diametrically opposed, with the rhetorical flourish of the Chorus set against the gravity and deep feeling of Williams's campfire musings. One of the things that we as audience members instinctively do when watching a play is work out who is telling us the truth and who is speaking from vested interests, from some other agenda, in order to convince us of something. If Williams isn't willing to let things go then neither is Henry, and he attempts to answer Williams's lengthy misgivings focused on the King's responsibility for bringing them to this juncture with an even lengthier speech refuting the King's responsibility for his subjects' souls. Who is telling us the truth here? Perhaps they both are, but that doesn't necessarily mean that, in the moment, we believe them both.

**141–81** Henry's response is almost four times as long as Williams's initial assertion. Henry could be taking his time and clearly laying out the opposing viewpoint on the matter; on the other hand, he could be bullying and overwhelming the other man into seeing it his way. The key is not so much in Henry's speech as in the tone and physicality of Williams's response according to the Folio text (ll. 178–9). Williams could speak this like a revelation, as if he has indeed now seen the light on this matter. Perhaps more likely, especially since the conflict between the two continues just ahead, is that Williams speaks this grudgingly, bludgeoned by Henry's relentless rhetoric into agreement against his better judgement. In that case, Bates could be trying to diffuse the tension or change the subject with his promise, whatever their doubts, to 'fight lustily' for the King in the morning.

**182–217**   But by this point apparently Henry and Williams just don't like each other, and they take the opportunity to argue about something else so that their encounter ends in a challenge to a quarrel or a duel or to some promised violence to come; the exchange of gloves betokens the commitment to finish this later. It doesn't really matter whose fault this is (although Henry, as he does with Pistol, at the least seems to egg it on) – what is most startling is that we see Henry in this situation at all. Whether it is designed to contradict the Chorus's earlier assertions about Henry's behaviour and its effect on his men, or meant to show a decidedly different Henry when his official self is not apparent, the encounter is probably not what we expected and certainly does not show Henry to advantage. By the end, Bates is the only one who speaks any sense: 'Be friends, you English fools . . . we have French quarrels enough.'

Is this scene a contrast with the earlier scene in the French camp or a parallel to it? Perhaps on both sides tensions are high, and men who should be comrades end up spending their energies fighting with each other and forgetting the enemy. There are a couple of other important physical choices available at the end of the scene. The Folio marks the exit of the three soldiers after Bates's last line; perhaps Bates is forcibly removing Williams so that the threatened violence between him and Henry doesn't break out here and now. If that is where they exit, then Henry is left delivering his next four lines to their backs – a slightly pathetic gesture especially if he has to shout after them, and a bit demeaning for a king, even if in disguise.

But the physical/visual wild card for perhaps the whole scene is Alexander Court, who says one line at the start of the scene and then is silent for the next 130 lines. On stage, a silent figure can be dramatically compelling – since he doesn't *say* anything, we start to wonder what he's *thinking*. He is the one most like us, listening, taking things in, weighing the arguments. The silent figure can, in subtle or strong ways, guide our responses to the action through his non-verbal reactions. He may simply indicate his agreement with his comrade Williams throughout, which might strengthen Williams's position and weaken Henry's a bit. Or, he could listen carefully to both, withholding his assent to either side – until he leaves. He might then give Henry a wink or a shrug, as if to say that his friend is always a bit of a hothead – such a gesture would let Henry off the hook a bit for what just transpired. But if Court stops and shoots Henry a dirty look before he follows his comrades out, or if he looks right through Henry during that somewhat forced 'French crowns' joke, shakes his head and slowly walks away, the effect could be devastating – a silent but palpable on-stage judgement of Henry where Henry is found wanting.

**218–25**  'Upon the King' begins the soliloquy we have been waiting for. This is our first chance really to get inside the head of this politician/rhetorician/leader of England. Considering how late it comes in the play, and how many times so far we would have liked to have known exactly what Henry was thinking, this speech has a lot riding on it for our understanding of and response to Henry's character. Over its 50 or so lines, we certainly get some sense of the weight of the world that Henry feels his public role consigns upon him. But the moment where Henry has us or loses us might come quite early, and be determined not so much by what he says as by vocal inflection and gesture in how he says it. When Henry says that the king is 'subject to the breath / Of every fool', he may be speaking generally or specifically. If generally, then this idea is part of a developing argument about the private strain of the public role. But Henry might also have someone specific in mind here (as these suggested directions could indicate):

> We must bear all. O hard condition, (*becoming increasingly agitated*)
> Twin-born with greatness: subject to the breath (*looking after Williams*)
> Of every FOOL (*he spits out the word in the direction Williams left*) . . .

If Henry seems to be referring to Williams as the object of his scorn and derision here (or later at lines 256–8), then we will have to judge whether, from what we've heard and seen, this accusation is justified, or if it just makes Henry look petty and vindictive. Similarly, as he goes on about 'what infinite heartsease / Must kings neglect that private men enjoy', if we think that by 'private men' Henry is referring to the three common soldiers he just argued with, then we might wonder what heartsease exactly they are enjoying, as they contemplate their own deaths by following the king's orders on the morrow.

**226–68** Henry's soliloquy has the potential to be deeply moving, revealing as it does the strain felt by the man under the role, under the 'ceremony'. On the other hand, after the very human concerns and straight talking of those three soldiers earlier, Henry's speech may come across as an extended whinge. If we are on Henry's side at this point, we may feel for the private man beneath the public mask; if not, his 'emotional' outburst may leave us cold. Certainly the rhetorical build of the speech is powerful, especially through the list of details that make up this 'thrice royal ceremony' (ll. 48–55), but the point of contrast to all this – the 'wretched slave' with a 'vacant mind' – creates a tricky moment. If Henry can make this unexamined life sound like a consummation devoutly to be wished, we'll get the point of the simplicity he yearns for. If there is even a hint of disdain or dismissal, we may be cringing instead. A compelling actor speaking unguardedly, simply and directly to us, can really pull us in here, but if we are inclined to find fault with special pleading about the burdens of the rich and powerful, we have plenty of opportunity. At any rate, we might recall that for all Henry's disillusionment (or whining) about 'ceremony', he has not got along very well in this scene without it.

**269–72** Henry's soliloquy ends on another point that requires us to make a judgement. If Henry has spoken to us directly through this soliloquy, if he has finally opened up to us as he has done for no one on-stage so far, if he has confessed to us honestly about the pressures he faces and the regret he feels for what is given up to be this thing called 'a king', then our hearts may well go out to him. At the least we understand him better – there is no rest for majesty, and he is the one who has to live with all the difficult choices made so that others can live in peace. On the other hand, we may remember all the times that Henry has shifted responsibility for his actions so far, and wonder what exactly still weighs on him. We may feel that Henry is not being 'real' here but using his rhetorical skills once again to sell a certain position, perhaps to himself as much as to us. If we resist, we might see the end of the soliloquy as the height of disingenuousness and hypocrisy – does he really think we will feel for him, when maintaining the peace apparently means starting a war on false pretences and dragging his countrymen overseas to be killed or to butcher others? The end of the soliloquy requires us not just to listen but to take a side.

**273 to the end** Erpingham's arrival doesn't seem to interrupt Henry as much as it allows him to change gear, and launch with new urgency into his prayer. If Henry gives Erpingham his cloak back at this point, then we also have a strong visual sense of Henry shedding his disguised state to be more himself – perhaps then we see the prayer, rather than the preceding soliloquy, as Henry at his most open and vulnerable. If Henry ends on a serene note, calm and quiet in voice and body, then we face a man who now accepts who he is and puts his faith in higher powers for the outcome of the day's events. However, if he ends in a state of heightened agitation or even despair – 'Though all that I can do is nothing worth' – then we may be watching a man wrestling through his own dark night of the soul and trying to make deals with God, with uncertain results. There is no time for Henry or for us to dwell on this – now Gloucester searches Henry out, and our audience with the private man is over.

## Act IV, scene ii

The cold night that looked grimly on the English camp is overtaken by the morning sun that shines on the French commanders. Several phrases – 'Do but behold yon poor and starved band,' 'we upon this mountain's basis' and 'Yon island carrions . . . ill-favouredly become the morning field' – imply that they are all gazing down upon the English. On Shakespeare's stage, the actors out on the thrust would have been looking down upon the groundlings, and this direct and prolonged disparagement of the 'poor and starved . . . shells and husks of men', the 'beggared' and 'lifeless' English, may well have been taken personally and so met with hisses and boos in response.

As Henry did earlier, the actors playing the French commanders can here make the audience into Henry's army; if the staging intent is to confirm French hubris and English underdog status, and to put the audience on Henry's side, then having the French look down on us, berate us, and sneer at us will likely do the trick. If not, the scene is also perfectly understandable simply as fighting men pumping themselves up before battle.

### Act IV, scene iii

**1–18**    The fact that the scene starts without Henry does two things. First, it allows us to see the men without their leader and therefore not just 'performing' bravery for their king – does their physicality match the French description from the previous scene? Secondly, it builds up some anticipation of Henry's entrance, considering the state we last saw him in – has he shaken off the dark thoughts of the night before; is he ready to lead these common men he envied and disparaged in his soliloquy; and how will he prepare them for what they are all about to face? The conversation amongst Henry's commanders may be played tense and fearfully, or with a kind of stoic resignation. The lines that provide the actual springboard for Henry's battle speech (ll. 16–18) might be spat out with deep frustration, bitterness, even despair; or be expressed in laughter, indicating anxiety rising towards hysteria; or be delivered with a quiet resignation to the sure doom that awaits. Whatever tone is taken with these lines, Henry will pick it up in order to rework it to his, and his army's, advantage.

**18**    Of course, Henry must enter early in order to hear these lines (the Folio suggests in the middle of line 16). There may be a certain tension in the crowd if others see him and fear his reaction. The early entrance, before he begins speaking, also allows Henry a moment to gauge his on-stage audience. He can indicate with a smile and a nod that he expected just such worries, and has a speech ready to counter them, or he could listen carefully, realize that everything lies in the balance now, and make his decision here, in the moment, about what he needs to say to them all. The first possibility shows us Henry the rhetorician, the leader with words at the ready to convince and cajole those around him. The second would set up an encounter with someone a little more human, a man on the spot who listens and then finds his way, moment by moment, to make a connection with those around him.

**19–39**   Henry doesn't counter the existential dread of men before a battle with specific strategies to survive, minimize their losses or even ensure they win, but with a shift of focus to something intangible – honour. Honour is what Henry offers all of them a share in. Henry's proclamation that anyone who's not up for the battle can claim passport out of here may be honest, or a purely rhetorical offer, or even a bluff or a dare. Henry's command of his audience may be measured in any pause that he leaves after the offer, or in the speed with which he moves on. There may be reactions from his men – are they tempted by this, do they flinch or glance nervously around at each other to see who wants to take it, do they think Henry actually *means* it, do some of them even leave, or do they all hold tight to hear the rest of Henry's argument? Of course, the rhetorical flourish that ends this section of the speech (ll. 38–9) is akin to saying anyone who even thinks of leaving is an unmanly coward (a notion Henry returns to at line 66).

**40–67**   The first section of the speech, on honour (about 20 lines), contains about sixteen pieces of major punctuation; the second section, the St Crispin part (28 lines), only has about nine. Even allowing for vagaries of punctuation in F and any modern edition, this is a huge difference, indicating a certain stop-and-start quality (and so hesitation? uncertainty? tension?) to the former and then a swifter, sweeping flow to the latter. The difference indicates Henry, mid-speech, rising to the occasion before us, by shifting from tense conditions in the present to a reassuring vision of the future – a future that, moments ago, none of the other commanders thought they had.

Henry's physical strategy with the speech is just as important as any rhetorical strategy. Perhaps he stands apart from his men to make his offer of paid departure, showing them the door in a sense.

If they don't all run out, he might take the opportunity to start
moving amongst them as he builds his argument. He might pick
someone out of the crowd to make his joke about remembering the
day's feats 'with advantages' to get a smile or laugh from them. He
might even move towards his commanders and touch or slap them
on the back as he names them. The key to his argument – the creation
of this 'happy few', this 'band of brothers' – implies that Henry does
not stand apart from or high above them, but is in the midst of them
as one of that band.

**68–78**    The end of Henry's speech may be greeted with shouts and
cheers, but Salisbury's sudden entrance with news of the impending
French charge offers an opportunity to see if Henry's speech has
made a real as well as a rhetorical difference. Perhaps the soldiers
whose physicality earlier indicated their tension and fear can now
indicate an attitude of 'bring it on'.

**79 to the end**    The entrance of Montjoy for ransom might threaten
to undo what Henry has just accomplished. Henry can either meet
him with the exasperation of someone who has to start all over again,
or he can immediately pounce on a further opportunity to display
the fortitude of the underdogs, and now right to the face of (this
representative of) the enemy. Certainly Henry picks up on Montjoy's
image of the English lying dead in French fields to create his counter-
image of an army of the dead still managing to wreak havoc. Henry
goes on to offer a contrast (or one last bluff) that, whatever the
outward appearance of Henry's army – and by Henry's own words
they must not look too good (ll. 111–12) – their 'hearts are in the trim'.
The soldiers may offer some proof of this, with the proud or just
calmly assured looks they give Montjoy. Their defiant physicality can
measure the distance they have come from the beginning of the
scene, if Henry's speeches have been successful. After Montjoy leaves
and Henry orders his men to 'march away', we have one last opportunity to see the difference Henry has made, if his men exit with an
energy and determination that was not apparent when they entered
the scene.

## Act IV, scene iv

**1–20**   The scene begins with a stage direction calling for 'excursions' – in other words, for some kind of fighting, or at least troop movement, that comes in and out of the playing space. This stage direction gives productions the permission to stage something of the main battle of Agincourt, and it could be filled with spectacle and violence. But the scene that Shakespeare goes on to dramatize is hardly the heroic action the play and Henry's pre-battle speeches might have led us to expect, and a lot more like that 'brawl ridiculous' the Chorus spoke of earlier. The battle of Pistol and Monsieur Le Fer is the only actual fighting between French and English that Shakespeare specifically calls for. It may be brutal or comical or even accidental, but something must happen at the beginning for the French soldier to find himself in the position where he must yield to Pistol. It might be a mock battle to see which coward flinches first – if the Frenchman gives up the moment he sees Pistol, it may indicate not only Pistol's undeserved good luck but also something of the unsuitability of the French soldiers drafted into this fight. On the other hand, a bit of brutality and dirty fighting might not be out of character for Pistol either, making this representation of Agincourt more ugly than honourable or ridiculous. Pistol then might either gloat over his triumph from a safe distance for most of the scene, or reinforce his power by administering a good kicking to accentuate each of his demands.

**21–58**   What is the Boy doing here? Is he a willing or reluctant witness to this scene? Does he back up Pistol's threats or does he attempt to intervene to prevent the abuse of a prisoner? Depending on our earlier thoughts about the Boy, we may be surprised that one of the Eastcheap low-life is fluent enough in French to provide simultaneous translation – this can be played for laughs against Pistol's crudity, but it will certainly raise the Boy in our estimations. Meanwhile, Pistol's continued threats eventually take him to his favourite French phrase, 'couper la gorge', and, presumably, a no-need-to-translate promise of such an event to come 'by this my sword'. Pistol's abated fury in the face of the promised 200-crown ransom is met by a gesture implied in the Boy's line 'He gives you upon his knees a thousand thanks.' If the French soldier was standing through the scene, he gets down on his knees to thank Pistol; if he has been the victim of a prolonged beating while prostrate on the ground after his capture, he may instead struggle through his pain to make it up to a kneeling position. The French soldier may be effusive, smiling, weeping, foppishly kissing Pistol's feet during his thanks, or he might maintain his dignity, and a simmering rage, by spitting out the words, perhaps as he spits out his teeth.

**59 to the end**     Pistol's 'Follow me' and the Boy's translation implies an exit for Pistol and the French soldier, and how it happens will probably complete the approach taken through the scene. Pistol could be keeping the Frenchman at a ridiculously safe distance with his sword (and so forcing the prisoner to go ahead rather than follow, or walking backwards so he might be 'followed' while keeping the sword between them), or might be dragging and kicking his prisoner, still on all fours, off the stage.

The Boy's soliloquy seems to indicate that he wanted nothing to do with this encounter. It also reveals to us that Nim has been hanged, along with Bardolph, for stealing. We don't know much about the rest of Henry's army, but the casualty rate among the Eastcheap gang is now at 50 per cent, and the Boy's rather foreboding comment that the French 'might have a good prey' of those guarding the camp hints that the number might go higher yet.

### Act IV, scene v

If we thought that Pistol's victory over M. Le Fer was an aberration or a joke, Act IV, scene v brings out the French commanders to tell us that the entire French army is being routed. A couple of strong choices are available for their entrance. Since this is more or less the same group that came out to look down their noses at the English in Act IV, scene ii, they might return to the same stage position, the difference now being the very different picture they see and paint for us – the repetition of the physical position would drive home the irony of just how wrong they were. Another possibility would be to have them stagger on, now lost in the fray itself, dirtied, bruised and bloodied. This change from their earlier pristine, high and mighty selves would be equally startling and ironic. There are further sound effects of the ongoing battle (line 5, SD) – violent enough, apparently, to drive someone to run from the scene (l. 6), be it either a passing group of soldiers or one of the commanders. The protest that they might still be victorious 'if any order might be thought upon' implies a certain amount of chaos on the stage, so a group of fleeing soldiers who cross the space would fit that bill. Of course, the following and immediately contradictory line – 'The devil take order now' – shows continued chaos amongst the commanders. Whether in defiance or in despair, at least some of the French commanders exit to (re)join the fray, while others may well be leaving in the opposite direction.

## Act IV, scene vi

**1–2**   The Folio indicates further sounds of battle to cover the shift from the French exit to the mass entrance of the English army with their French prisoners, one of whom, presumably, is Le Fer, being led by Pistol. A choice has to be made here about the state of the prisoners: whether they are somehow shackled or tied together, or if they are disarmed but free to move, with their hands on their heads and guarded at sword-point. If the rest of the prisoners are bunched together, Pistol may be keeping Le Fer, and the ransom he represents, just to himself. Henry's opening lines indicate either a strategic retreat, or a quick regrouping (to deposit the prisoners somewhere?) before rejoining the fray, which only gets interrupted with other crucial news.

**3–34**   When Exeter joins Henry to relay verbally the lengthy story of York's and Suffolk's deaths, there is plenty of stage time to relay physically the state of the French and English soldiers. The English may be energized by their success so far, or exhausted and on the brink of collapse despite early victories – the news of two commanders' deaths could either be sobering, disheartening, or just the thing to rouse them to revenge (depending on Henry's reaction, it could be part of what spurs his violent order momentarily). The French may

be defeated and downcast, or observing their captors with disdain
and even looking for an opening to escape.

**35 to the end**    Either the new alarum indicates, or Henry sees (off
stage), that 'The French have reinforced their scattered men,' which
leads to his order to kill the prisoners (ll. 37–8). Since French prisoners
have specifically been brought out on the stage, since there are armed
English guarding them, and since Henry's order is so simple and direct,
something has to happen here. It is one thing for Henry, as commander, to maintain his cool and issue an order that will keep victory in
sight by preventing his outnumbered troops from being overrun; it is
quite another to see it being carried out. If the French prisoners are tied
up or have clearly given up, and none of them understand English
enough to catch the order given, then we might just be watching a
massacre at Henry's behest, perhaps even as he looks on. If the French
are free to move, and if they understand what Henry is proposing, they
might try to fight back before being cut down. Historically, some of
Henry's men deliberately disobeyed this order – perhaps as Henry
marches off there is some hesitation, or even outright refusal, by some
soldiers. In the Quarto, Pistol's phrase 'coup la gorge' indicates that he
cuts Le Fer's throat and, the loser ever, gives up his ransom.

## Act IV, scene vii

**1–10**    If there were prisoners killed on stage, they could be dragged
off in the shift to the next scene, but this is theatrically counterintu-
itive – if we understand that the prisoners had to be killed to free up
those guarding them for further fighting, it makes no sense for those
guards now to be occupied hauling corpses around. Perhaps a
tarpauline could be thrown over the pile of corpses, which would
then become the dead bodies of the boys, which Gower and Fluellen
refer to. Gower's assertion (l. 5) confirms any fears we may have had
at the Boy's exit from Act IV, scene iv, but his further point (ll. 8–10)
bears some scrutiny. Whatever Gower thinks he means, we know
that Henry ordered *that* massacre independent of *this* massacre. By
Gower's reasoning, Henry may be justified, but we have seen it can
only be in retrospect.

**11–49**   If Gower and Fluellen were emotionally shaken by what they saw, they seem to get over it in time to clear the way for a prolonged discourse on Alexander the Pig, the geography of Wales and Macedon, rivers with salmons, and the demise of a former friend of their king. For us, it is one more opportunity to see these men talking and not fighting. But if Shakespeare chooses to interrupt things now, in the middle of the battle, there had better be some significance to their talk, and their discussion forms one more crux in our response to Henry. Fluellen, speaking as he often does in 'figures and comparisons', relates a story of the drunken Alexander killing his best friend Cleitus in a rage. Gower interrupts: 'Our King is not like him in that. He never killed any of his friends.' We may feel that the play has shown us something different, even if Fluellen pushes on to make not a comparison but a contrast (ll. 40–5).

Is the story supposed to be flattering for Henry? Are we supposed to consider the difference between acting in a drunken rage and acting in right wits and good judgement, as far as killing (whether bodies or just hearts) is concerned? We watched Henry make a cool, calculated decision to kill all the prisoners for the greater good of keeping his men at the advantage: are we being invited to read the rejection of Falstaff as something also for the greater good, even if somewhat inhuman? We already know that Falstaff is dead, apparently because the King killed his heart, and we also know that Henry ordered the execution of his former bedfellow Lord Scrope, and ordered the execution of Bardolph. In light of these 'facts', should we think of Gower's defence of Henry as ironic because obviously false? Perhaps it is ironic and *true*, because the Eastcheap gang might have thought they were Henry's friends but were just being used for a time (as Henry always planned to cast them aside) and Lord Scrope was just someone for the King to make an example of (after all, we neither see nor know anything of their relationship until it's over). We might also take Henry's side in seeing it as true: Falstaff *et al.* were just parasites on and not real friends to Henry; Bardolph deliberately disobeyed orders on the campaign; and Scrope was of course a false friend and traitor. We might even take this further if we bought into Henry's soliloquy the night before battle: a king is a public, ceremonial construction, and can never have anything like private friends.

This is a lot to turn on a single line, but the moment invites it – the action stops in its tracks here, and the conversation invites us to consider Henry's character and any judgements we've made about him so far. And then, on cue, Henry enters.

**50–60**   He enters in anger, presumably about the massacre of the boys, and the threats he asks to be conveyed 'unto the horsemen on yon hill' (are they the killers?) sound something like his threats before the walls of Harfleur. Of course, this time when he talks of cutting prisoners' throats, it is neither bluff nor rhetoric, as we have just seen such action carried out in front of us.

**61–82**   Before any English herald can exit to deliver this ultimatum, the French herald enters. Gloucester's observation that Montjoy's 'eyes are humbler than they used to be' implies a downcast physicality upon entrance. Henry might be too angry to notice this, or perhaps he does and suspects a trick – in this state he might be almost attacking Montjoy, and Montjoy might quickly complete Henry's last line in self-defence to stop the onslaught. Montjoy has a reason to be humble, as he brings news that the French are giving up, confirmed in no uncertain terms (l. 81). If the other members of the English army on stage have been waiting in anticipation, they may erupt in cheers at this news – if so, the hard stress and plosive consonant that begins Henry's 'Praised be God, and not our strength, for it' may be designed to cut through any celebration and instil respect and awe in his men.

**83 to the end**   The naming of the battle may be a formal, even reverential moment. Fluellen's slightly comic, if not slightly inconsequential, historical comparison and anecdote may be there just to fill the stunned silence. The gentle jibe about Henry being an 'honest man' is juxtaposed with the entrance of Williams – a man Henry was neither very honest nor very honourable with the night before. In case we miss this point, the rest of the scene – many lines and much stage time – is taken up by Henry arranging a little trick whereby Fluellen will answer the challenge, and get the 'box o'th' ear' that was meant for Henry. This may just seem like some comic relief, especially if we think Fluellen is a windbag, and wouldn't mind seeing someone smack him. It may, after the talk of Henry being an honest man, just seem dishonest, not to mention frivolous in its timing. Henry dispenses Warwick and Gloucester to make sure things don't get out of hand, but only after setting up a practical joke that might feel more appropriate to a locker room (and his old self?) than these very recent killing fields.

## Act IV, scene viii

**1–23**   It doesn't take long for Henry's practical joke to play out and for Fluellen to get struck on the head by Williams over the glove he wears. Gower tries to rush to his friend's defence – Fluellen's 'Stand away, Captain Gower' implies as much, and that Fluellen wants to handle this himself. But a few lines later Fluellen is asking for the help he just refused (ll. 17–18), implying that he either backs down or is physically rebuffed or even incapacitated by Williams.

**24–70**   Henry enters to undo the comic confusion he has created, and we can easily just read this little episode as blowing off a bit of steam after the battle while we're waiting for the lists of the dead Henry asked for in the previous scene. Or it can be played, and we can read it, as another unflattering episode for Henry's character. Henry reveals his identity from the night before, but his wording – 'It was ourself thou didst abuse' – may sound a bit like the pot calling the kettle black. In his defence, Williams develops exactly this point, at length – if there was any fault, it was Henry's. If Williams speaks with some moral authority here, rather than with the red-faced bluster of someone just made the butt of a royal joke, then Henry's offer of the glove full of crowns may seem less generosity or a way to make things right than an attempt to buy him off, especially if Williams sees it for what it is and refuses to accept. 'I will none of your money' may refer to Fluellen's meagre contribution in imitation of the King, but it could also refer to the glove full of money that Exeter is trying to get him to take. If Williams refuses Henry's gesture, then the whole moment sits rather awkwardly, and the arrival of the death lists saves Henry from the slow death of his little joke.

**71 to the end**     When Henry names those of the French nobility on
the death list, we may be reminded of the French King's great list of
French nobles in Act III, scene v – although the echo is a grim one. In
terms of numbers, and stage time in its relating, the list of English
dead is shockingly meagre. But before we can think about how this
could possibly be – what was the English strategy, how unprepared
were the French, just how many prisoners were massacred after they
gave up? – and perhaps even before we can consider if 'None else of
name' undoes the 'band of brothers' rhetoric from before the battle,
Henry ascribes this incredible disparity in victory to God and God
only. Again, depending on how we feel about the man, we can see
'Take it God, / For it is none but thine' and 'God fought for us' as
either Christian humility or as one last evasion of personal responsibility for bloodshed. Henry calls for *Non Nobis* and *Te Deum* to be
sung, and perhaps that is what we hear as the stage clears – presumably in solemn fashion with no English gloating, high-fives or even
smiles, after Henry's stern order (ll. 112–14).

# ACT V

## Act V, Chorus

The Chorus reappears now to hustle us, Henry and the story across
time and space, and for once makes it clear from the beginning that
it is filling in a gap that will not be dramatized at all. Before Act II,
the Chorus promised not to make us seasick with so rapidly
moving the story across the channel, but there is at least something
comic if not queasy about the way we are whipped around now (ll.
6–9). The Chorus offers us descriptions of an English landing that
we won't see, a triumphal entry into London that we won't see –
although assuring us that Henry does it with great humility – and a
short stay in London that we won't see, so moving us and the story
'straight back again to France'. The Chorus freely admits to just filling time (ll. 43–4) so an actor playing the Chorus will most likely do
it quickly.

## Act V, scene i

**1–12**  If the Chorus wants to move us right back again to France, this scene begins as if we never left, in the middle of a conversation – 'Nay, that's right' – between Gower and Fluellen over some slight, this time involving Pistol. In Act IV, scene vii, Fluellen talked about the proud tradition of Welshmen wearing leeks in their caps, and the lines here (1–2, 10–11) imply that this is what Fluellen now does. Whether he looks proud or ridiculous probably depends on the size of his leek.

**13–47**  When Pistol enters, at least he thinks Fluellen looks ridiculous – 'art thou bedlam?' – but Fluellen reveals that the leek is not for decoration but for Pistol to eat. Quarto supplies a stage direction that Fluellen begins beating Pistol into submission after 'There is one goat for you.' Another blow might be implied on 'there is sauce for it' – either a continued beating will be the metaphorical sauce that convinces Pistol he is hungry, or perhaps Fluellen has drawn blood, which is now, rather gruesomely, the literal sauce that drips on the proffered leek. A further beating might be implied by Gower's cry of 'Enough' or perhaps Gower physically holds his friend back in mid-blow. Gower says that Pistol is 'astonished' by the beating, so perhaps stunned or at least incapacitated, and not just surprised. Fluellen indicates where those blows have been falling – on Pistol's 'pate' or 'coxcomb', i.e. head, which is indeed now 'ploody'. Pistol threatens revenge, but the abrupt change to 'I eat and eat' implies either a further threat from Fluellen or another blow, as does Fluellen's sarcastic question 'Will you have some more sauce to your leek?' If we wondered while reading how or why Fluellen was able to get the advantage of Pistol so quickly and thoroughly, Pistol's plea for him to 'quiet thy cudgel' (l. 47) tells us why. This is not a scene of fisticuffs, *mano a mano*, but a scene of one man repeatedly beating another with some kind of weapon. It really depends on our personal tastes, as much as on the brutal or slapstick staging, whether we find this kind of thing funny.

**48–72**  Fluellen makes sure Pistol eats every bite – 'Nay, pray you throw none away' – and then offers him a coin to help him heal his wounds. If Pistol at first resists – 'Me, a groat?' – then Fluellen ensures he takes it by threatening to bring out of his pocket another leek for eating. If from his breeches or trouser pocket, the image becomes more ridiculous and a bit obscene as he stands before a presumably kneeling Pistol. If it is a huge leek and very bulging pants and a most humiliated and open-mouthed Pistol, again depending on our tastes we might find the image quite funny. If the playing focus is on Fluellen's coin rather than his crotch, we may start drawing comparisons with an almost identical sequence we saw earlier, where Henry played out a practical joke on a man at his mercy and ended it with a cash payment (which Fluellen imitated there as well). We might see Fluellen's version as a pale and silly reflection – lower comedy than the King's not-quite-high comedy routine. We might also think that, with or without a phallic leek swinging about, both incidents are just male games of the whose-dick-is-bigger variety.

**73 to the end**    After Fluellen exits, and after Gower rubs it in a bit, Pistol is left alone with us. If we have been laughing at the leek spectacle, Pistol's revelation that another friend has died reminds us that, despite the miraculously small number of English casualties, the attrition rate among Pistol's circle is running very, very high. Our emotions might get tossed around a bit, from laughing at Pistol to feeling sorry for him and then, perhaps, to being a bit frightened of him, if we see him in a larger context as dissolute survivor. His hardening into bitterness – 'from my weary limbs / Honour is cudgelled' doesn't sound like the credo of a happy-go-lucky loser – and his plans to become a bawd and thief upon returning to England show us two things. First, that once again what the Chorus says and what Shakespeare chooses to dramatize don't match up, as the Chorus told us of returning to England, celebrating, and going back to France, and of a big jump forward in time, while the scene itself seems never to have left France, is about settling scores rather than celebrating victory, and occurs apparently just after the battle. Secondly, that Henry's all-inclusive band of brothers doesn't hold up for long, with in-fighting, class struggles and ethnic rivalries among the English, and with Pistol so clearly destined to fall through the cracks of any postwar society, a reject of this great victory and glorious time.

## Act V, scene ii

Scene ii gives us what the Chorus promised – Henry's return to France. The mass entrance brings on a great assembly of important personages, but very clearly divided into two camps. The French enter from one door in the original stage directions, the English from another, but a production must decide how far they advance towards each other. The two sides may go on to speak cordially or at least diplomatically, but the greater the physical space between them, the higher the degree of discomfort, distrust and disdain beneath any soothing words. In his formal greeting, Henry reveals that it is Burgundy who has brought the two sides together, perhaps implying that, although the stage directions indicate that Burgundy enters with the French, he takes his place on the stage somewhere between the French and English delegations.

1–22    Much will be revealed in the way the opening lines are delivered. Is Henry courteous, smug, gloating or businesslike in the delivery of his first speech? It would be very easy – and either very funny or bitterly ironic – for the French King to deliver 'Right joyous are we to behold your face' sounding anything but joyous, but if so is he seething or utterly despondent? And does Queen Isobel, a character we meet for the first time here, adopt a conciliatory or accusatory tone when she talks of now beholding Henry's eyes whose looks previously have killed so many of her countrymen? There may be many formal bows, stiff nods or ostentatious flourishes between the two sides – 'We do salute you . . . I do salute you' – but that probably stops when Burgundy begins his formal mediation.

23–67    The two sides may continue to stand far apart, leaving Burgundy in the middle trying to bridge that physical gap with his rhetoric. Burgundy might literally bring them (l. 26) closer to each other, perhaps to take seats 'face to face' across a council table of some sort. Perhaps we are willing to accept a certain amount of verbosity with our diplomacy, but Burgundy's 44-line speech painting France as a disordered garden may stretch our theatrical patience – especially since, unlike the Salic Law speech early in the play, which promised to *launch* the action, this speech comes very late and is about *stopping* further action. Perhaps Isobel's comment about Henry's murderous eyes is a bit too honest, and any talk of what has transpired between English and French is better cloaked in metaphor, the more elaborate and extended the better. But for all of Burgundy's poetic diplomacy, his speech can still contain a dramatically effective sting near the end, in the form of an accusation, bitter recognition, and even a threat (ll. 56–60). He might be saying to this soldier king that soldiers are savages, or saying to both sides that any desire for further contests in the field would be savagery, or saying that Frenchmen in this wild garden are now thinking only of bloodshed, and so raising the spectre of uprisings and insurgencies against any occupying power. If Burgundy builds the speech to a strong climax here, his vision of an 'unnatural' world may make both confident winner and livid loser break their gazes.

**68–76**   If Burgundy ends on a note of some moral authority, Henry appears to be neither shamed nor drawn by it; instead he simply points out that peace is literally 'in your hands', i.e. in the treaty (or articles of surrender) that Burgundy and/or the French King hold. If Henry wanted to be particularly brazen (or tough-minded) here, he might pick the papers up off the table and put them back in his opponent's hands as he speaks, as his material counter to Burgundy's verbiage. The existence of these articles of treaty – written up, here and apparently in hand – calls into question what Burgundy thought he could have achieved with his fine speech. Unless, perhaps, it was more directed at the stubborn French King than at Henry. If Burgundy adds a sigh of weariness or even a pointed touch of sarcasm to his line about the French King's lack of response 'as yet', such an internal struggle would become clear.

**77–98**   The French King's response to being put on the spot about the treaty is to leave the room. He must stand to leave, or make some kind of gesture to indicate his desire to do this elsewhere, in order to prompt Henry's lines about his men going with the French King and his question about whether the French Queen will be staying. But when Henry asks (demands?) that Catherine stay behind, we may get the idea that this mass exit was pre-planned, to give Henry a chance to be alone with the young woman who comprises his 'capital demand'. A variety of responses can be signalled as everyone else files off – winks and bemusement from Henry's men, expectancy from Catherine's mother, even some animosity from the French Lords, who might resent the daughter of France being sold to this English victor.

**98–101** The scansion might indicate that Henry begins his lines quickly, as he finishes Queen Isobel's exit line – perhaps he is anxious to get down to this business. A production could also use a long pause here. If Henry stands grinning inanely, or suddenly loses his nerve and shuffles about bashfully for a moment while the two ladies look on expectantly, then the pause would be comic and would serve to introduce us to the underdog of love. If, however, Henry sits back and regards her with a smug smile, or if he looks her up and down in a predatory fashion, then his gaze and the pause it fills become that of the victor sizing up his spoils of war. Henry might maintain a respectful distance, beginning his suit formally, perhaps even with a bow, or maintain a distance but begin to prowl around her, coolly evaluating her responses. Perhaps he barges right up to her in a less-than-suave manner, or perhaps as he looks at her he realizes and is taken aback at how beautiful she is, necessitating the repetition of 'fair' in his first line.

**102–21** Catherine's initial response, that she is at a linguistic disadvantage here, may be a confession, or it may be something of a tactic allowing her to plead ignorance while she goes about evaluating him – after all, her conferral with Alice over Henry's 'angel' line would seem to indicate that her understanding is not unduly handicapped. This is crucial to our perception of how the scene unfolds. A pretty but uncomprehending Catherine who just smiles helplessly while Henry speaks at her – at length – is a very different partner, in this scene, from a Catherine who, under cover of translation delay, is watchful and aware as she weighs Henry's behaviour and his suit. Similarly, Henry's perfect translation of Catherine's 'langues des hommes' comment seems to indicate that he is not so very bad at understanding her language, either.

**122–31**   When Henry offers to speak more directly and to 'clap hands' immediately on a bargain between them, Catherine's 'me understand well' implies that she comprehends not just his words but also his tactic of trying to rush to a conclusion for the sake of simplicity. If at the beginning it registers with us that the scene cannot simply be about two people who just don't comprehend each other, we will begin to wonder what else is happening, and what then is at stake, in this longest of encounters between English and French in the entire play.

**132–73**   In his next speech, Henry talks about leap-frog and saddles and jackanapes and sunburns, all in the course of protesting that he has 'no cunning in protestation' and claiming he is not one of 'these fellows of infinite tongue', in a speech that is some 33 lines long. If anyone strikes us as a plain speaker here it will be Catherine, whose one-line reply – 'Is it possible dat I sould love de *ennemi* of France?' – rather cuts to the heart of this encounter. Henry may be taken aback at this, or in his response he could acknowledge that she will be tougher to convince than he thought. He might laugh at her direct-ness while turning her question into his little joke about loving France so much he 'will not part with a village of it'. After his circular yours-and-mine word game, Catherine's incomprehension (l. 173) may be asking not for the *translation* Henry goes on to provide but for an *explanation* of exactly how conquering and killing her people is supposed to show his love. Again, a Catherine played as alert and aware will call into question the content and intention of Henry's suit, not the foreign language in which he makes it.

**174–84**   Depending on how we feel about Henry, and directed by Catherine's reactions, his attempt to 'conquer' the French language may seem charmingly awkward, a moment of frustration (since he is used to getting what he wants), or even distasteful and disingenuous. It may provoke delighted laughter from Catherine, as Henry's last line could imply, or this mock display of effort may provoke Catherine to call him on it by coolly pointing out (ll. 183–4) that she already knows – as the scene has already shown – he speaks perfectly serviceable French.

**185–235**    As the scene continues, the crux of interpretation again is not in Henry's many lines but in Catherine's few lines – 'I cannot tell . . . I do not know dat' – which means either she doesn't comprehend Henry's *language*, and so leads Henry comically into ever greater feats of trying to make himself understood, or she doesn't understand Henry himself or go along with what he is trying to accomplish here.

On the page, we tend to read the wooing scene on Henry's terms, since he has the overwhelming majority of the lines from which we are getting our information. When he hopes she can understand at least a little English, we assume that's the (comic) dilemma. When he talks of her laughing we assume she does. When he tells her to put off her maiden blushes we assume she has been blushing. But on the stage, the source of meaning in the scene is much more balanced, with Catherine's physical presence, positioning and gestural choices as well as her few but pointed lines carrying just as much weight as Henry's incessant speechifying. On the stage, we will look to Catherine to decide whether or not she is blushing, and if those blushes are from anger and humiliation rather than the coyness Henry chooses to ascribe to her. On stage, Catherine may choose not to find Henry very charming, funny, royal or attractive at all, and so we may have to adjust our response to him accordingly. The fact that the scene is so long may be due not to earnest wooing or comedic language hurdles but rather to the fact that it is here Henry meets the most sustained resistance of any encounter in the play.

**235–66**    A knowing Catherine who resists Henry's charms can turn one of their most important exchanges from a tentative coming-together into a stark and ironic reminder that her consent to Henry's love-suit is immaterial when Daddy is in the next room selling her off even now as part of the English demands. Her response can indicate not a surrender but a clear-eyed recognition of the way things really are. When Henry offers to kiss her hand, Catherine refuses: Henry should not abase himself, she argues, by kissing the hand of one so far beneath him. Coming from the daughter of a king, we may feel that slightly overstates the social status issue, but coming from the daughter of a defeated king, and as the representative of a defeated people, and to their conqueror, Catherine's reasoning may make more sense, and may be much more politically pointed than socially demure. When Henry instead offers to kiss her lips, he is told that is not the way things are done here. Henry's reply, essentially, is that things have changed (ll. 260–2). But it is of course her custom, the custom of her country, that is being broken, and Catherine must accept that 'patiently and yielding'.

**266–71**  The kiss can be confirmation of Henry's victory in love and the coming together of these pretty young things, or it can be the final bit of bullying in a protracted battle. Henry's request for her to act 'patiently and yielding' can be gentle and seductive, or it may come across as an order. And, of course, the physical gesture of the kiss may be mutual, or he may have to take it from an unresponsive partner. When the larger French and English parties return to the stage, they may walk in on two kids smooching, or they may walk in on a stand-off. When the others return, Catherine does not speak again.

**272–310**  The banter and innuendo between Burgundy and Henry may be witty or crude, depending on how we feel about Catherine's fate. If the preceding sequence has been played as a coming together, then Henry's comments about love not appearing 'in his true likeness' will seem like teasing; if the keynote is resistance, then we will hear frustration and perhaps, almost, an admission of failure in this campaign for Catherine's consent. Henry may be throwing up his hands when he asks Burgundy to 'teach your cousin to consent winking' precisely because he has *not* got a clear-eyed Catherine to 'wink and yield'.

**311 to the end**  But if Catherine has not entirely yielded, the French King does, as Henry and Catherine both knew he would. He gives Catherine to be Henry's wife, 'consent[ing] to all terms of reason' and 'grant[ing] every article' save one that Henry, in three quick lines, persuades him to add. On stage, we can literally watch the peace being bought with the exchange of Catherine as so much currency changing hands – 'Take her, fair son.' The French King, the French Queen and King Henry all talk of marriage, peace and unity to come from this arrangement. The stage picture can reflect this with a mingling of those who previously were on opposite sides of the stage, or it may show some strain and lingering unease if that separate space is maintained. The tension may be palpable, and threaten seriously to undercut the settlement, if the Dauphin is among the 'other French' and appearing on stage to witness his own disinheritance. Henry may try to eclipse any physical oppositions or continuing tensions by moving with Catherine to the front and centre. His final couplet encompasses the entire on-stage audience, and rings out over them and us:

> Then shall I swear to Kate, and you to me,
> And may our oaths well kept and prosperous be.

## Epilogue

And here something very curious happens. The Chorus, who through the entire play has acted as head cheerleader for Henry's character and his actions (even when the action Shakespeare chooses to dramatize seems to point in another direction), steps forward to contradict the hero. The Chorus tells us that the oaths will not be well kept, and the outcome of Henry's efforts will be less than prosperous for himself, his heir and his country. The Chorus, who has spent the play talking of Henry's greatness and the inadequacies of the author, the stage and the company to portray it, now speaks of Henry's coming failure while praising the success of Shakespeare's theatre in having already presented it (in Shakespeare's earlier-written but chronologically later tetralogy of history plays). Like so much before, there are a couple of ways we can take this: that we have been watching a glorious highpoint in English history, so glorious it cannot last, so we should bask in this glory while we have it; or, that all this has been and will be for naught – a tough lesson, perhaps, for a play in which we have been regularly encouraged to invest ourselves by 'piec[ing] out imperfections with [our] thoughts'. The Chorus has urged our complicity in the theatrical project as well as Henry's historical project, but this final Chorus marks a parting of the ways: between ourselves and the performers; between our complicity and their efforts; and between theatrical triumph and historical failure. It will depend on our responses to all the cruxes thus far whether we 'read' the final Chorus as a somewhat bittersweet coda to action of great merit and glory, or as an unexpected theatrical deflation, or as the final lesson and logical outcome of Henry's attempted hypocritical glossing of providence, honour and necessity over brutal actions and bad faith.

# 4 Key Productions and Performances

We can look at so many moments in *Henry V* and say, 'Well, there are a couple of ways things can go here.' Of course, if there were only one way things could go, one inherent and recoverable meaning, one clear and definitive authorial intention and hence only one way of performing any particular line or action, then it wouldn't be much of a play, and it wouldn't have much of a life in the theatre. Performance is not a derivative action, or just the echo and shadow of meaning that is textually immanent. In fact, what is textually immanent is performance. A playscript remembers past performances – the material and social context the playwright has experienced leading to this piece of writing – and anticipates (and incites) future performance – the material and social life of this piece of writing when it comes to be performed. A text of a play is the site of possibilities, not the seat of final arbitration. Performance is the place where decisions are made that make the present meaning of the play.

Some moment-by-moment choices will register more strongly than others in creating the 'meaning' of the play. I'll be looking at five different stage versions of *Henry V*, from 1984 to 2003, and focusing on some specifically inflected moments in performance. These inflected moments can be of piercing psychological acuity, or a stunning visual *coup de théâtre*, but they are the definitive moments where the production shows its hand, as it were. They do not necessarily correspond to the most textually obvious places – the Folio's fairly innocuous stage direction calling for '*other French*' in Act V, scene ii, is taken by the English Shakespeare Company to include the Dauphin, and his reaction to his disinheritance creates one of the most striking sequences in that production. Cuts are the most readily discernible

meaning-manipulations for a textual analysis, but as the 1984 Royal
Shakespeare Company (RSC) production shows, you can leave in the
apparently problematic episode of Bardolph's execution and still
turn it to Henry's advantage in the way the moment is staged.
Performance decisions create the strongest local meanings.

The key inflected moments that follow tend to reveal the terms
upon which a production engages us. Is the play about Henry: should
we like or dislike him? Is it about his actions: should we approve or
disapprove of what he and his men do? And is it about them or us,
and how: is our experience of the event and its meanings contained
within the theatrical presentation by actors of a historical past, or
does the play spill into the world around us now, and if so are we
observers or are we part of the problems the play raises? The 'couple
of ways' Henry V can go have often been articulated in performance
criticism in terms of an 'official' or pro-Henry version of the play's
meanings and a 'secret' sceptical version. But the secret has been out
for quite a while now, and with so many contradictory elements in
the playscript to be struggled with, by artists and audiences, there
really is no official interpretation.

## Royal Shakespeare Company, 1984

The 1984 RSC production of Henry V with a 23-year-old Kenneth
Branagh is perhaps now mainly thought of in terms of its ambitious
young star's precocious classical debut, and for being a springboard
of sorts for Branagh's later film version of the play. It's only simplify-
ing things a bit to say that the RSC staging presented us with the grim
realities of warfare and a Henry we could like if we chose to, while
Branagh's film went on to utilize the grim realities in such a way that
we could only end up liking Henry even more. Unlike Branagh's film,
whose realistic effects are skilfully created and carefully controlled to
ensure intense personal engagement with Henry and investment in
his story, this stage version, directed by Adrian Noble, was more
objective, open and ambivalent. This is not surprising, given the
number of contradictory impulses at work in its creation.

The production was the first at the RSC in ten years, and the first following the 1982 Falklands War. That conflict cost 255 British and 655 Argentinian lives; it brought down the military junta of the losers, and ensured the previously unpopular Margaret Thatcher a huge majority in the 1983 British election; and it became a cultural flashpoint for British thought about war, nationalism, heroism, waste and, for some, about the art of busying giddy minds with foreign quarrels. A British production of *Henry V* would inevitably be seen in this light, even though both Noble and Branagh were reluctant to let the obvious contemporary parallels and concerns (in Branagh's words) shackle, burden or prove 'reductive to the work' (*Players of Shakespeare 2*, p. 98). This attitude towards the relationship of art and society seems diametrically opposed to Nicholas Hytner's goals for his production 20 years later.

Branagh had just finished playing St Francis of Assisi, from which he brought an interest in a 'spiritual vocabulary' directly into his work on Henry. He and Noble agreed to explore and play up the contradictions and paradoxes of a character that Branagh characterized as both a man of '*genuine* humility and piety' and a 'professional killer of chilling ruthlessness'. Branagh believed that the character had 'huge reserves of compassion' and 'a genuine visionary quality' and though he was interested in the darkness of things like the Harfleur threats he believed that Henry's 'capacity for extraordinary compassion and forgiveness are self-evident in the rest of the play' (pp. 97–8). Unfortunately, Branagh doesn't specifically state what those other self-evident moments are, or how compassion and forgiveness square with things like invasions and executions and killing prisoners. The inflected moments for his psychological portrait of the King were things like the 'moral *gravitas*' of weighing the decision to go to war, the 'tremendous sense of hurt' over his betrayal by Scrope, and a 'solitude so painful' that it produces the 'Upon the King' soliloquy. He even arranged an interview with Prince Charles to get a better sense of what it feels like to be a monarch. As is the right of the actor creating it, this is a highly individualized characterization that, for all it professes interest in paradoxes, leans pretty heavily in one idealized direction – not surprisingly for an excited young man with a lot on his shoulders. In Branagh's writing about the role, and about his 'intense journey' through it, contradictions become less important as the rhetoric heats up about spiritual depths. When Branagh writes that Henry is 'a man who saw far beyond individual actions, assessing their often terrible consequences, and *feeling* them as a man' (pp. 100–1), one might be tempted to add the phrase Branagh forgot: 'but then he goes ahead and does them anyway'.

Noble talked a conservative directing game, professing to take Shakespeare on his own terms with a humanist eye to characters' journeys from chaos to harmony, and eschewing any sceptical Brechtian overlay onto the complex emotional and moral life of the plays (Loehlin, pp. 85–6; Berry, *On Directing*). In directing *Henry V*, Noble stripped the RSC mainstage down to bare planks and brick, used rough, natural materials for costumes, bright lighting and visible instruments, a white half-curtain pulled by hand across the proscenium, and provided a cool, sardonic, even alienating Narrator/Chorus to run the show – all rather textbook Brechtian staging techniques. The avowed humanist but practising Brechtian is a strange beast, and perhaps not inappropriate for this paradoxical play. Loehlin believes that the dissonance and diametrical opposition of Branagh's earnest Henry on his deeply felt spiritual journey of personal growth and transformation, against Ian McDiarmid's caustic Chorus and the other anti-illusionist/anti-idealist staging techniques, is precisely what generated the production's power (pp. 88–90).

One of the key inflected moments for this production was the death of Bardolph, which provided the first-half finale. Bardolph was brought out by Exeter to kneel facing his former friend across the wide expanse of the downstage apron, while the rest of the army stood upstage under pouring rain (cleverly draining off through the grated metal floor beyond the proscenium line) and the Chorus looked on from the side. After a long silence, Henry gave a signal and Exeter slowly and gruesomely garroted Bardolph while Henry fought off tears and tried not to break. Branagh wrote that this was an 'unsentimental' moment, but in his understanding it was a 'test of Henry's character' that he had to pass to continue on his spiritual journey: 'Bardolph must die but not, I felt, without intense personal cost to the king' (*Players of Shakespeare* 2, pp. 102–3) – with personal cost but not, somehow, with personal responsibility. In the emotional life of the play, as opposed to its clinical and critical physical staging, the death of Bardolph was something very important that happened to Henry, rather than something Henry ordered, sanctioned, signalled, watched and approved of.

The end of the play was staged in an equally contradictory fashion. The dead of Agincourt were left upstage after the battle, as the half-curtain was drawn to set up first the Pistol scene and then the French court scene in front. After the Pistol sequence, people entered upstage behind the curtain to light candles for the dead; lit from behind, the half-curtain became semi-transparent, and the flickering image of the dead and lost remained visible through the brighter forestage scene of political settlement, wooing, wedding and reconcilement (Loehlin, pp. 102–4; Hodgdon, p. 209).

The use of the transparent half-curtain here transformed the stage space into a visual palimpsest, where the content of the previous scene was not erased after the action moved forward in the story. The half-curtain is a standard Brechtian device, multiplying performing spaces to allow for a dialectical confrontation between concurrent actions and images. A standard linear staging practice would tend to resolve the opposition created through juxtaposed episodes by literally sweeping one element away into the wings to set up the next. Here the audience was left to deal with the juxtaposition and resolve the opposition, since the staging kept the detritus of the battlefield locked together with the peace, settlement and wooing. Every line and every gesture of the scene had the battlefield dead as its backdrop. When the Chorus came forward into a follow-spot in front of the court and couple at the end, there were actually three simultaneous stage spaces plus the direct recognition of the audience space, further heightening the confrontation of disparate visual elements. There was a coolly ironic commentator with some bad news in the spotlight, his arms outstretched to embrace the audience in special pleading and/or acknowledged complicity, with golden couple and 'reconciled' enemies behind him in silhouette, and fallen bodies on the field in the candlelight behind the curtain. The clever Brechtian technique – each scene for itself, but here all visible at the same time – created a moment as visually powerful as it was emotionally and

morally dissatisfying. The staging bunched up incompatible
elements at the end, and audiences would have to resolve the contradictions by confronting the power structures and social imperatives
that work to bring such a thing to pass – in the play, in history, in
human relations. Unless, that is, an audience was already drawn into
personal identification with the star turn and spiritual journey of the
winning, personable, likeable young fellow in the lead role – something Branagh the director takes great pains to ensure for Branagh
the actor in his later film version.

### English Shakespeare Company, 1986–9

With their newly created touring company and brash, maverick,
pissed-off (politically and artistically) attitudes, director Michael
Bogdanov and actor Michael Pennington were not afraid to take up
the post-Falklands banner Noble and Branagh were ambivalent
about. Their initial English Shakespeare Company (ESC) tour was of
*Henry IV, Parts 1 and 2* and *Henry V*, grouped together under the collective title *The Henrys* (at the end of 1987 *Richard II*, the *Henry VI* plays and
*Richard III* were added to a larger enterprise called *The Wars of the
Roses*). The ESC was formed to tour 'accessible Shakespeare', which
meant, for Bogdanov, a specific way of creating theatre: 'I'm trying to
give the public a company that knows, every time it's on stage, what
it's doing, what it's saying, why it's there, how every single character
and every single line fits into social and political structures' (Berry, *On
Directing*, p. 224). The emphasis on social and political structures may
be thought of as Brechtian or Marxist; in practice, it meant that the
focus of the playing was on making the situation clear, rather than on
a character's spiritual or emotional depth, back-story, transforma-
tional journey, etc. The social and political emphasis, the focus on the
situation, meant that Shakespeare's histories became 'plays for today,
the lessons of history unlearnt' (Bogdanov and Pennington, *The ESC*,
p. 24).

A 'situation' like the departure of the Eastcheap crew for the war
became in this production a strongly inflected, hugely effective
moment bursting with theatrical energy and political critique. As the

men said their sad goodbyes to the Hostess, the pace slowed, emotions ran high, the pauses were human and awkward, and all was accompanied by a sappy Spanish guitar (playing 'I Did it My Way' very slowly – perhaps a slight hint of the Thatcherian critique to come). The men turned and started to move downstage, the Hostess wept and waved as she disappeared upstage. Then the four men launched into a rousing chorus of ''Ere we go, 'ere we go, 'ere we go' while 'Jerusalem' blasted over the speakers and a great crowd appeared on the upstage catwalk, cheering, shouting, working noise-makers, waving flags and unfurling a giant banner that read 'Fuck the Frogs'. As this was going on, the Chorus crossed the stage with a giant placard reading 'Gotcha!' Medieval invaders of France as pumped-up football hooligans, historical imperialism reframed by the *Sun's* infamous headline about the sinking of the *General Belgrano* by 'our lads' in the Falklands War – Bogdanov made the theatrical, historical and current situation perfectly clear. Apart from the political critique in the contemporary parallel, the 'Gotcha' was also for (and of) the audience. If we had been feeling sorry for this bunch, and thinking of war in terms of husbands and wives separated or the fears and anxieties of the common folk, the image reminded us that they are also looking gleefully forward to kicking the shit out of people. But even if we blame them for that base impulse, we're also reminded that, stirred up to such mindless jingoism, they are doing exactly what Henry and his council want and need them to do. There was no getting sentimental about the situation – we needed to consider where actions fit into social and political structures.

Similarly, the killing of the prisoners became very important, not for its insight into Henry's mind or for its psychological effect on those carrying out the order or even for the pitiable spectacle of unarmed men being cut down, but for its commentary on the use-value of human beings in war. Fulfilling the promise of the earlier football chants, on the battlefield Pistol was running rampant. For Bogdanov, this was the battle of Agincourt: 'Pistol kicking the shit out of a wounded Frenchman' (Bogdanov and Pennington, *The ESC*, p. 47). While Pistol kicked M. Le Fer in the crotch and at another point grabbed and twisted his testicles, the keynote wasn't turning the noble and heroic into the sordid and dirty but playing up the acquisitive side of warfare. Pistol was racing about the battlefield with a shopping cart, looting corpses, picking up whatever he could grab to sell later. When M. Le Fer bargained for his life by promising a handsome cash ransom, Pistol simply lifted him up and dumped him in the shopping cart with his other loot. The imperial expedition was about getting other people's stuff and greedily commodifying the personal – a notion this production revisited in the more-mercantile-than-romantic final scene with the King and his 'capital demand', Catherine.

But what M. Le Fer's life was worth was not his or Pistol's to negotiate and decide – it was up to Henry. When Henry gave the order to kill the prisoners, it was a matter-of-fact decision, a quick weighing of the options. The order was passed on by Henry's commanders, and though Pistol tried to hide Le Fer's face under his helmet – 'Prisoner? What prisoner?' – he was threatened at gunpoint (a gesture that echoed Henry himself threatening his men back to the breach at Harfleur by waving his machine gun at them from the top of a tank) until he slit the Frenchman's throat. The killing was not a shocking or emotional moment – Le Fer was unconscious in the cart, and Pistol just seemed really disappointed about losing the man's cash value – but the political and social structure dictating the action was clear. War is about acquiring another country and its people. It is commanders who decide what lives are worth, and soldiers kill or die.

In part because they were doing the *Henry IV* plays as well, Bogdanov and Pennington decided to take Hal/Henry at his word from his first soliloquy: 'I know you all . . .'. Bogdanov thought of him as 'determined [and] cold' and Pennington concurred: 'What I was after for [the character] . . . was a combination of this chilly political clear-sightedness with a wayward, unstable quality in the moment' (Bogdanov and Pennington, *The ESC*, p. 49). The only concession to an emotional reading Pennington allowed himself was that 'what is strong in *Henry V*, and very actable, is that his sense of mission has cost him his youth, ease and spontaneity' (ibid., p.50). The wooing of Catherine was certainly not marked by either ease or spontaneity; lovely and intriguing as she might be, he always knew (as did she) what he was there for, and knew that he would get it. That was his attitude to the French court throughout the play – brusque, efficient, determined, so that even the gruesome threats before Harfleur had a 'take it or leave it, and don't think I'm joking' off-handedness to them. In the final scene, with a tight smile and impatient physicality, he simply wouldn't take no for an answer on any point, even if that meant causing Clyde Pollitt's soft-spoken French King extreme discomfort as he was forced to accept the wording of his son's disinheritance while his son looked on. By having the Dauphin a wordless but physically crucial presence in the scene, Bogdanov again meant to keep the action's place in the political structure clear. When Henry had wrung the last request out of the French King, he stepped forward to Catherine to 'kiss her as [his] sovereign queen', at which point the Dauphin bolted upright, knocked over his chair, and stormed off. Henry then stormed away from Catherine, threatening to throw a bit of a wobbly, and it was only the carefully delivered intervention of the French Queen that brought the final moment back to an uneasy peace. Her words were not celebratory but delicately diplomatic. The final Chorus did not step forward to contradict the scene of happiness so much as to confirm the bad feelings that had just broken through it.

How important are intentions, at the end of the day? How does it help *Henry V* or its audience that in 1986 Michael Bogdanov was very angry about social and economic policies that promoted and rewarded greed and exploitation, about a senseless war of expediency that played on the basest of jingoism, about the spread of English football hooliganism? For this audience member, who, at the time, knew little about Thatcherism, less about the Falklands War, and nothing about Heysel Stadium, a day spent with *The Henrys* on their tour to Toronto in 1987 was still filled with exciting, vital theatre where everything seemed to be up for grabs.

## Royal Shakespeare Company, 1994

The Royal Shakespeare Company's 1994 production of *Henry V* in Stratford-upon-Avon, directed by Matthew Warchus with sets by Neil Warmington, imagined the play as an act of remembrance. It began with a roped-off exhibit of a robe of state on a dressmaker's dummy. The Chorus was an old man, a war veteran wearing a poppy in his lapel, and 'our guide to some kind of "Agincourt Experience"' in a 'museum specializing in lifelike tableaux of historic events' (Jackson). A crowd of on-stage museum-goers occasionally bore witness to these carefully arranged still images – *The King Decides on War* (with the English Court in full support), *The Fleet Embarks* (with Henry as noble leader), *The French Imagine their Victory* (with English soldiers fallen and cowering beneath horses' hooves), etc. The images were often very striking, but there was something elegiac rather than particularly vital about them, as if remembrance also implied reverence. In fact, the stage floor itself was revealed – at the start of the battle of Agincourt, when the hydraulics suddenly raised the back to form a steep rake – to be Henry's tombstone, with his name and the dates of his life, 1387–1422, carved into it.

But the crucial inspiration for the design of the battle of Agincourt came straight out of Williams's speech about 'all those legs and arms and heads chopped off in a battle'. The back of the stage was left open to the cyclorama, upon which were projected stylized clouds. Pennants on tall poles were placed at the back of the rake, rising up directly in front of the cyclorama. Legs and arms and heads hung down on chains of various lengths above the back of the rake. The body parts were actually pieces of plate metal armour – disconnected metal encasements for hip and thigh, for shoulder and arm, even a steel helmet and visor for the head – but the link to Williams's image was unmistakable. The image was at first very startling. It did much more to convey the realities of medieval battle, with its stabbing and hacking and the resultant detritus of such close and brutal encounters, than any of the carefully choreographed sword fighting which actually took place on the stage. The hanging pieces remained in place until, after the list of the dead was read, Henry called for 'holy rites' and for *Non Nobis* and *Te Deum* to be sung. At that point, as the music played and the action was halted and the assembled English army watched, the pieces slowly rose up into the flies.

Bringing the legs and arms and heads lost in battle into the stage picture was a potent reminder of the fears of dismemberment and of not dying well expressed on the eve of the battle. Having the legs and arms and heads lost in battle ascend heavenward accompanied by choral music praising God seemed meant to account for those severed limbs and answer those fears in the most positive manner possible. 'Fall to rise,' the image said, promising salvation to those who had given their bodies in their King's just cause, providing a sense of spiritual closure to this great fellowship of death, and offering to re-member what had been severed, dismembered and dispersed. But the relationship of this image to the debate before the battle that inspired it seemed problematic. The image of ascending body parts does not necessarily respond to the debate so much as cancel it out. 'Fall to rise,' the image said, where before Henry had argued that even a good cause promised no such thing, that the King's cause in fact had nothing to do with salvation. 'Fall to rise,' the image said, for even pieces of men can go to heaven and be positively accounted for in the afterglow of righteous victory. The juxtaposition of stage-floor-as-tombstone with the hanging limbs suggested that hacked bodies were Henry's true legacy, but their heavenward ascension let him off the hook.

This image also seemed to beg the question as to exactly whose pieces these were. Before the battle Henry says that war is God's vengeance, war is a kind of judgement, and after the battle Henry claims that God fought for the English. If God fought for the English, it only stands to reason that God fought against the French. If war is judgement, then the reading of the lists of the dead shows an extraordinary number of French soldiers were judged and found wanting. When the music began and the body parts were raised, only the English were on the stage. If Henry is right about God's bias, it must be only English body parts ascending. By the same token, earlier when the French prisoners were slaughtered, they fell and rolled down the raked platforms to the downstage floor. For a modern theatre with the very latest technologies, there was something distinctly medieval about this vertical (and judgemental) staging: heavens above, hell below, English up, French down.

The handling of this key image, in keeping with the overall elegiac tone of the production, suggested that we should support those who went to war, and remember and honour their sacrifices, at the expense of debating why they went, judging the King who led them to it, or engaging with the disturbing reality of what these soldiers were asked to do for Henry's victory and our theatrical satisfaction. The sense of the play's action as 'History' for remembrance trumped its potential for visceral impact or rigorous debate in the moment.

## Globe Theatre, 1997

If it is visceral impact we want, then the opening production in the new Globe Theatre, reconstructed on Bankside in London, provides an interesting test case for what this play can do in performance. This *Henry V* invited, and one might argue relied upon, a much stronger interaction between actors and audiences, and its visceral impact had nothing to do with blood and gore and shocking images of warfare, but with the experience of heightened audience participation that the new/old architecture seemed to create.

The reconstructed Globe Theatre exists somewhere between being an experiential museum and an experimental lab based around period performance conditions. Its operative mode exists somewhere between re-creation and discovery of how old plays work in the type of space for which they were written. Pauline Kiernan refers to the Globe's paradoxical effect as 'the shock of the old', and she documents how, by working in the space, 'actors and audiences began to discover how the physical characteristics of an early modern public amphitheatre could influence the respective roles of the actors and the playgoers in the performance space' (pp. 3–4). Kiernan argues that being subjected to period performance conditions in the inaugural season led the company to many revelations and discoveries about period performance practice: about men playing women, about listening versus seeing, about the best patterns for blocking and the strongest positions on the stage, and the most successful ways of handling entrances and exits. These are all performative elements, and they say things about the experience of a play in performance, but what do period performance conditions say about a play's meaning as created in performance? Here another element comes, literally, into (the) play: Kiernan, along with every other commentator on the first productions in the new Globe, recognizes a more important, more vocal, more powerful role for the audience in this space, in making the meaning of the experience. There has been a lot of debate about 'authenticity' and what that might mean for players at the Globe and audiences who go to it. The painstaking, detailed historical reconstruction of the theatre space, coupled with the rigorous adherence to original practices such as men playing the female roles, rushes on the stage floor, thoroughly re-created period clothing, etc. for such productions as the 1997 *Henry V*, can't help but imply something of a recovery of 'the way it really was' for the resultant experience. Expectation also creates meaning in performance, and the Globe sends some pretty strong signals its audiences often pick up and run with. For audiences of *Henry V*, this translated at times into 'a kind of self-conscious pantomime-style audience participation' where 'cheers and boos at the English and French ... seem like a jokey game at let's-pretend-to-be-jolly-Elizabethans' ('Intimate Magnificence'). The actors may have allowed and encouraged it, but the reaction seemed to come from expectations of what this experience was all about; the audiences 'had the impression that this would have been the "Elizabethan response" at such [moments], and they were obligingly supplying it' (Cordner, p. 211). The question is how much audiences were there for *Henry V* and its performance as opposed to a somewhat different, perhaps parallel experience, the performance of 'Being at the Globe'. A related question, of course, is how performers of the first, deal with and integrate the second.

To consider performer choices, dictates of the space, and the audience's role in the action for creating meaning, I'll look at just one example, although a crucial and complicated one. When he delivered the lines of 'Once more unto the breach,' Mark Rylance as Henry addressed his on-stage soldiers and also his audience in the house. The playgoers, surrounding the actor and clearly visible to him and to each other, readily became the English army. The speech became *for* them and about them, not just a story delivered to them, and the audience responded with shouts, words of encouragement and assent, cheers and applause. But moments later, when Henry came to deliver his threats to the Governor of Harfleur, the relationship of actor and audience to material changed. 'During his delivery of the

ultimatum outside the gates of Harfleur . . . Rylance was positioned
directly under the governor, out of his sight line; Rylance used the
oratorical threat of violence to win submission while simultaneously
displaying postures of exhaustion to indicate to viewers that Henry
was bluffing, his troops incapable of successfully assaulting Harfleur'
(Marshall, p. 359). This is an interesting performance experiment and
discovery given the conditions of the Globe stage; with the governor
on the balcony and Henry directly below on the stage floor, Henry
could send his voice and words up to one focus of attention, and his
gestures and physicality out to another, conveying one meaning to
the on-stage character and another to the audience in the house. But
only one meaning was the 'real' meaning:

> Rylance inched his way through the speech improvisatorily, with recur-
> rent glances at his supporting commanders, as if for inspiration for
> further horrors with which to intimidate the French. Then, on its last
> words, he looked once again at his comrades and smirked jovially at
> them. We were to understand that the whole thing was a ruse, a jape, a
> fantasy that was sure to dupe the credulous French, but which there was
> no actual risk of the good-hearted English carrying out.
>
>                                                        (Cordner, p. 212)

A potentially difficult moment becomes a great in-joke for the audience's sake – 'those silly Frenchies, they'll believe *anything*!' – and it
also lets the newly recruited audience/army off the hook from being
implicated in some of the more unsavoury aspects of warfare. What
gets generated is laughter at the French character's expense rather
than some other visceral response – discomfort, queasiness – at the
audience's expense. It was a performance 'discovery' in the space but
also a particular use of the audience that said: 'I'm going to talk about
fighting on and being brave and winning the day, and I want you to
imagine you are my soldiers; I'm also going to talk about rape and
murder and infanticide, but I don't want you to imagine doing those
things.' It is okay to recruit audiences to 'play soldier' but not to
recruit them to 'play rapist'. Is this simply good discretion, or a tactical evasion of what the play can do in a space that relies heavily on
complicity for its effects – both enjoyable and uncomfortable?
   One could argue that the 'Globe Experience' and its increased

audience participation in the moment ensured that the content of *Henry V*, and its presentation, were simply not about us or about today. The play was about historical figures and a historical battle – for all the jeers and hissing, the performance of jingoism, there were no reports from the Globe of gangs of English audience members beating up and violating French tourists after the show. Its performers were just actors – responsive audiences weren't applauding war and carnage, they were applauding an actor playing a character who delivered an effective speech. Perhaps we have come to expect too many searching subtleties or grand statements from this play in performance now, and it takes some old architecture, *ersatz* authenticity and a boisterous audience to show it. Cheering on the heroes, hissing the bad guys – perhaps that is the visceral reaction the play wants and deserves, where neither the 'official' nor 'secret' versions of the play are as important as having an enjoyable time in the theatre.

## National Theatre, 2003

Early in his tenure as the new Artistic Director of England's National Theatre, Nicholas Hytner was looking for a great and complex national epic for his mission of 'reflecting the nation back to itself'. He wanted an old play 'that might connect specifically to today' but when he chose *Henry V* he 'had no idea we'd be rehearsing it when we invaded Iraq'. Hytner certainly thought of the play in terms of the geopolitical moment when nations like the US and UK 'felt that it was right and morally urgent to intervene in a military fashion in other countries'. For Hytner, 'the play was illuminated by current events' and he hoped his audiences also found 'current events illuminated by the play' (Stagework, Director). The production was very popular, and almost all of the critics commented on how deeply resonant the play was in sounding the current debate between imperial aggressions and the moral quest for the right.

The production was in up-to-the-minute modern dress, and many key moments were filtered and replayed through television monitors at the front of the stage, to comment on how contemporary media are embroiled in the business of selling, spinning and waging war.

The Chorus came across as Henry's press officer or personal assistant; the end of Act I, scene ii became a Prime Ministerial address to the nation; the threats before Harfleur were captured by a reporter with a camera, although Henry motioned to cut the feed when he got to the really nasty bits; the early portions of the Harfleur footage reappeared with French subtitles for Alice and Catherine to watch before her English lesson; and after Agincourt a slick propaganda video was aired with waving flags, inspirational images of Henry leading his troops, and set to a hip, confident but still reverent song with a recurring chorus of 'We fank ya, Lord, for victory.'

There were many striking moments, even aside from the often uncanny contemporary parallels and clever media manipulations, all tending to undermine a heroic or patriotic understanding of events. Adrian Lester's Henry himself executed Bardolph, with one shot to the back of the head. When Henry gave the order to kill the prisoners, his men all refused, leaving only Fluellen to obey the direct order and mow the prisoners down himself. After the wooing sequence, Catherine refused to take Henry's hand for the 'official' public announcement of their impending marriage, and the two left the stage separately at the end of the scene.

The most interesting of inflected moments concerned the treatment of the Chorus, played by Penny Downie. To make sense of the Chorus in the contemporary context, Hytner originally thought of her as perhaps a very right-wing journalist or war reporter; this evolved into what Downie called a voice that was 'unquestionably pro-Henry in the way that some female journalists are completely in love with their subject'. Downie came to think of the Chorus as 'someone you and I'd meet in the Victoria and Albert Museum' who had become a bit 'myopic and one-sided' about her subject, 'a type of person who would be very pro-the-historical-fact of the man, and slightly unquestioning'. The Chorus wants a hero figure, and wants to believe in him, and wants to tell people about that belief. The play, and Henry's story, became framed by the story of the Chorus as a character who did not stand apart from the action but was forced to change with it. For Downie, 'both [the Chorus] and the audience go on a journey together' that took them from sparkling historical record through the disillusioning actual events portrayed on stage.

The Chorus was involved in her own battle, where 'she keeps presenting the positive line, but there are doubts', about which she continually has to say, 'Well, I'll let that one pass.' By the end, the Chorus had to face the fact that the story was, in Downie's word, a 'bloodbath' – as displayed now, with Bardolph's execution and the killing of the prisoners, and in the future, with civil war in the *Henry VI* plays to come (Stagework, Chorus). The action of the play was refigured as the story of the Chorus's disillusionment, even betrayal. In its historical moment of the invasion of Iraq, this story of disillusionment became even more resonant when memos emerged showing that the invasion was decided on well in advance, when it became obvious there were no weapons of mass destruction, and when a 'Mission Accomplished' photo-op bannered over continued chaos and bloodshed. It certainly all made sense. The play and the times fit together so well that it may be difficult to discern which was the hand and which was the glove.

Unfortunately, it may also be that the deepest irony of this production lies not in its sharp, contemporary, critical attitude to current events and to the old 'official' version of the play, but in an underlying theatrical conservatism. For all its obvious relevance and its bells and whistles of ironic, post-modern staging, the production may just be showing us what we already know: of course politicians lie; of course momentous decisions are made for vested interests; of course patriotism and war get packaged and sold to us in the media; of course people die for no good reason. In a sense, our easy recognition is just another way of (intellectually rather than viscerally) cheering on the things we like and hissing what we don't. When a production shows us what we already know, our experience of it becomes self-contained. We are not compelled to do anything about it, because the 'truth' is that's the way things are. A production can foreground an unjust war, and fabricated intelligence and propaganda, and bad faith – so do the newspapers. Henry still wins at Agincourt – Tony Blair and George Bush still get re-elected. The clarity and contemporaneity of this production ensure we get the message, but the self-satisfaction of 'getting' *Henry V* so fittingly dressed in the trappings of its social moment may lead us to nod our heads knowingly and go home, instead of being thoroughly shaken

down and left in a quarrelsome mood with the play, the performance, ourselves and the world. Of course, our experience of *Henry V*
and the meanings we take from it depend on what we want and
expect from the theatre; I would just suggest that it might not be to
anyone's advantage for this prickly play to 'make sense' in performance.

# 5  The Play on Screen

Shakespeare on screen is much more efficiently and ubiquitously transmitted than Shakespeare on stage; it is also, of course, not the same thing. Watching a film in a cinema can be a social experience, but our reactions make no difference to the production and the performances, so the experience lacks the more complex complicity involved in attending a theatrical presentation. When making a film it is easier to control the information the audience receives; with camera placement, shot choices and editing, a film director can tell us exactly what to look at, how to look at it, and for how long, in a way that any theatre director would envy. But that control also negates parts of the story. In the theatre, our eyes maintain a sense of the whole ensemble, even when we are drawn to a specific action or speaker at a specifically inflected moment. Since no film is made with a still camera locked off in a long shot, there will always be life outside the frame that goes unregarded as select moments are privileged and intensified. One could argue, though, that film's ability (through editing) to move swiftly from scene to scene is closer to the episodic structuring and rapid shifts in location that Shakespeare called for than is the tradition of pictorial staging with detailed sets but often interminable scene changes. Once the film is transferred to DVD or videocassette, it's the viewer who gains a level of temporal control that neither theatre performance nor cinema screening allows. We can take advantage of this for more careful analysis of specific moments and effects – to scrutinize exactly *how* meaning is made rather than just going along for the ride.

The four readily-available film and television versions of *Henry V* offer some instructive contrasts, from the overarching areas of

interpretive intentions and production style to the moment-by-
moment decisions the different principal actors make with the same
raw material available to them from the playscript behind the
screenplay. In broad terms, Laurence Olivier's 1944 film is the most
fanciful treatment, a royal pageant-play for film, with the self-
consciousness of its framing device as a performance in
Shakespeare's Globe, its bright and brilliantly coloured, two-dimensional *Très Riches Heures du Duc de Berri* sets for the French court and
its spectacular (and almost entirely bloodless) medieval re-enact-
ment of Agincourt. The 1979 BBC/Time-Life television version is
perhaps best described as the most dutiful screen rendering, with
almost all of the scenes and lines intact if not exactly inspired in
their staging and delivery. A multi-camera videotaped record of a
live stage performance, the 1989 English Shakespeare Company
production of the play as part of their series *The Wars of the Roses* is
by far the most sceptical version, where directorial and acting
choices strive to create a context within which the workings of
power might be seen, critiqued and judged rather than subsumed in
the unfolding and unquestioned action. Finally, Kenneth Branagh's
1989 feature film is the most personal version, an often close-up
account of what it feels like to be Henry.

    To some extent what follows consists of reviews, but it is the *vari-*
*ety* of choices made and the *implications* that follow upon those
choices, not necessarily the quality of their execution, that are most
instructive here. Whether the acting or staging is 'good' is to a great
extent in the eye of the beholder and historically or contextually
contingent. Olivier's contemporary status as a screen idol and his
contribution to the war effort are unaffected by feelings, now, that
his acting might be hammy and choices vapid, and thinking the BBC
version dull makes no difference to the thousands of undergradu-
ates who have gratefully viewed it just to get a better handle on the
action and who's who in it. The primary focus is on choices – those
things that the play can be made to do, when produced. I'll look at
each version in turn, then subject a couple of key moments –
Bardolph's death and the wooing of Catherine – to more extended
comparisons.

## Olivier, 1944

From the beginning of England's war with Germany, I realize now, I was being tuned up for the undreamt-of film of *Henry V*. As I flew over the country . . . I kept seeing it as Shakespeare's sceptred isle. . . . I had a mission; I was physically and emotionally very fit . . . my country was at war; I felt Shakespeare within me, I felt the cinema within him. I knew what I wanted to do.     (Olivier, pp. 185–6, 190)

What Olivier did was make what many feel is the first 'real' Shakespeare film. Released by the Ministry of Information from his duties in the Fleet Air Arm so he might serve the war effort in other ways, first-time director Olivier shot the film from the summer of 1943 to the summer of 1944, and when the film opened in England not so long after D-Day, it was dedicated 'To the Commandos and Airborne Troops of Great Britain, the spirit of whose ancestors it has been humbly attempted to recapture'. With a context this important, and a mission so clear and deeply felt by the director and star, it's no surprise that the message and meaning of the story would also be clear: the storytelling is heroic, stirring, patriotic, straightforward. Anything not easily played that way is cut.

When Olivier took the role of Henry at the Old Vic in 1937, he 'started by completely undercutting Henry' and 'fought against the heroism' because, at that time, he felt 'the whole atmosphere of the country . . . was against heroics' and he was firmly a part of that 'highly debunking generation' (Olivier, pp. 58–60, 252). The director, Tyrone Guthrie, convinced Olivier instead that heroic playing would be the only way to 'carry the audience' (p. 61) along with him in the big speeches. When the war started two years later, Olivier felt he was carrying the fate of the nation along with him, and two 'heroic' speeches from *Henry V* were his vehicle. Olivier visited military camps with a one-man show 'geared to whip up patriotism', and made good use of the St Crispin's Day speech, since

> by now I knew how to pace it all perfectly and was able slowly to whip up my wartime audience of real soldiers, urging them forward with me. . . . During the applause [for the St Crispin speech] I would hold my gesture and remain still. Then, when I felt the applause reach its peak and begin to

wane, I would launch into 'Once more unto the breach . . .'. By the time I
got to 'God for Harry . . .' I think they would have followed me anywhere.
Looking back, I don't think we could have won the war without 'Once
more unto the breach . . .' somewhere in our soldiers' hearts.     (pp. 64–6)

Olivier and egotism were not unknown to one another, but he clearly
felt, and tapped into, something of the power of those lines for that
audience at that time; he then took that knowledge and applied it to
the much broader message-delivery device of the cinema.

With a message and a mission, Olivier the screen idol but novice
director had to find the film grammar to take the Elizabethan play
into its new medium: 'The main problem, of course, was to find a
style which Shakespearean actors could act and yet which would be
acceptable to the audience of the time, used to little other than the
most obvious propaganda' (p. 186). Olivier might be implying that
his film was to be *sophisticated* propaganda, but certainly his aesthetic
choices in bringing the play to film are as distinctive as, and consid-
erably more varied than, his message. The film is also about the act of
filming Shakespeare.

The film starts with a playbill floating out of blue sky to announce
a performance of Shakespeare's play (*The Chronicle History of King
Henry the Fift*) in Shakespeare's theatre (the Globe) in Shakespeare's
time (1 May 1600). After tracking across a scale model of 1600s
London, Olivier plunges us into the 'real' set of the Globe, complete
with house band, orange-girls, ale sellers, and cod-Elizabethan actors
who perform in broad and declamatory style for their very responsive patrons. At first glance, this stylistic choice may not seem particularly innovative, but Olivier gives us a hint of where things are going
when the Chorus, as he savours the words and strides the boards and
works the house, suddenly steps forward towards the camera and
into a medium close-up. He delivers his request, 'On your imaginary
forces work,' directly to the camera and in a more normal speaking
voice, and for a moment William Walton's score is heard instead of
the boisterous house band. The Chorus is soon playing to his Globe
audience again; Walton's music soon fades out, but that brief
moment makes us aware of a contemporary filmic self-consciousness behind the apparent historical and theatrical immersion.

The broad style continues into Act I, scene i, with the clerics playing in arch comedic fashion. After a brief camera trip backstage
between scenes, ending with Olivier as Elizabethan Actor as Henry V,
coughing and clearing his throat before going on, Act I, scene ii is
played with the same exuberance – and exuberant crowd reactions.
The actors playing Elizabethan Actors playing Medieval Clerics play
Laurel and Hardy, turning the Salic Law section into slapstick. Papers
fly, places are lost, the King and nobles can't get a word in edgeways,
and one of the most problematic sections of the play passes by in
gales of audience-in-the-film laughter. Once the silliness is done,
Olivier, or rather the Elizabethan actor he is playing, begins to warm
to the part of Henry, and after deftly handling the Dauphin's insult he
gets a huge round of applause from his in-the-film audience. Act II,
scene i returns to silliness with the Eastcheap gang showboating with
grimaces and gags even though rain starts to pour down on them and
their Globe audience.

If we start to wonder exactly how long Olivier the director is going
to keep having all this (tiresome) fun in Ye Olde Globe, then all is
unfolding according to plan. Olivier 'wanted the film audience to get
a restless feeling of being crabbed and confined in the Globe's
wooden O, irritated by the silly actors speaking in their exaggerated
way' (p. 188). When the Chorus takes us to Southampton, Olivier the
director delivers us from the Globe and into an obviously two-
dimensional, painted pop-up village, but one where Olivier the actor
begins to speak 'realistically and with a modern tone' (p. 188). The
next scene, the second with the Eastcheap crew and following on
Falstaff's death – added to the film through speeches from *Henry IV,
Part 2*, with the dying man finally crushed under the remembered
words of Henry's rejection – is serious, understated and, since no
longer just a provocation for the in-the-film audience, actually quite
moving. The picture-book style introduced for Southampton is
picked up and magnified for the French scenes, where Olivier's
second design concept – 'something artificial, very pretty and unreal,
yet real to the mind's eye's vision of a romantic tale of an heroic medi-
aeval king' – and playing style – 'I wanted the characters to spring out
from the beautiful, stylized, almost cut-out scenery, alive and kicking
and speaking in vigorous and varied language' (p. 188) – take hold.

Whether the French court (or the English invaders, aside from Henry) are ever any more than two-dimensional accoutrements of their pretty, painted, two-dimensional picture-book sets is a matter of taste. Certainly Olivier doesn't help the French cause by making the French King rather batty and prone to sitting on the floor. When Exeter delivers his message to the French court in Act II, scene iv, the scene ends with the distracted King's line 'Tomorrow shall you know our . . . [*long pause, staring open-mouthed into the air*] mind at full,' and when he is told Henry has already landed in France, he faints. The Dauphin, in perhaps a passing topical reference, is strapping, blond and Teutonic in look, but rather fey in vocal styling and body language. The softening of the characters goes for the English side as well. Any potential for conspiracy and bad faith in Act I, scenes i and ii, is drowned out by the slapstick. The four national captains seem a good-natured lot. It is especially hard not to smile at Fluellen with his twitchy eyebrows and moustache, and MacMorris is not allowed seriously to disrupt the camaraderie, being played as a dreamy depressive, first shouting then pouting then weeping, and without animosity. Pistol's leave-taking near the end, a potential sour note, is delivered too archly to be very dark, and he stops to steal a pig and a chicken – O, that rascally Pistol! – on his way out.

Half the lines are gone, including: Henry's potentially nihilistic comment about breaking France all to pieces; everything regarding the three conspirators; the entirety of Henry's threats before Harfleur; everything about Bardolph's plight, Pistol and Fluellen's fight and Henry's decision from Act III, scene vi; the passage about Richard, usurpation and inherited guilt from Henry's prayer; the entire scene of Pistol and Le Fer; the order to kill the prisoners; all the glove business with Henry, Williams and Fluellen; the names of the French dead; Henry and Burgundy's off-colour jokes about Catherine; and the bad news contained in the final Chorus. Most of the cuts seem obvious considering the wartime context – no treachery at home, please, and we don't need to see our leader wracked with guilt, and for heaven's sake don't tell us our great victory soon just falls apart. But Olivier is also good at subtly pointing what remains to make the passage of the action even smoother. Following his victory at Harfleur, Henry gazes out over the countryside, and through the editing that gaze is taken to Catherine. After her language lesson, she too gazes off as if back to Henry – 'it is as though fate, and film technique, are drawing them together' (Loehlin, p. 38). Olivier takes Henry's prayer, gently delivered rather than a struggle through some dark night of the soul, only as far as 'Pluck their hearts from them' (IV.i.280). When his brother comes for him, Henry smiles, and the smile indicates he's ready, he knows what must be done, and he's looking ahead, not backwards now. Because of the smile, it is no surprise when we see Henry the next morning, relaxed, calm and confident, ready for the St Crispin's Day speech where he leads his men through the camp, and where his words are punctuated by vocalized outbursts of assent from the men to his winning appeal.

Agincourt marks Olivier's third stylistic shift. The fields are so green, the tents and banners and costumes so bright, that we might be forgiven for doubting their reality, but if the location is real the choreography of the battle itself is highly formal and missing one key colour. The only blood Olivier shows is a daub of red across the face of a boy ambushed at the King's tents. The response is a chivalric, one-on-one fight between Henry and the Constable where Henry wins the day decisively but bloodlessly. Agincourt is certainly 'filmic' – couldn't do it on stage, no mistaking it for low-budget television drama – but also of its time, as the whole film is, whether in the Globe or popping out from an illuminated medieval manuscript or charging through lush fields. It is a Technicolor wonder with a handsome leading man who can inspire confidence, lead graciously, and defeat the enemy with one blow. It is good entertainment, and a compelling fantasy for anyone who, sitting in a London movie theatre in 1944, would wish to think about it in terms of the world outside.

The film was commercially successful, and Olivier won a special Academy Award for Outstanding Achievement as Actor, Producer and Director. Olivier remained pleased with his earliest 'Shakespeare on celluloid' project: 'Not quite a film, not quite a play, Henry V on screen was a new form of entertainment, an exuberant concoction made (with love) to show that this great playwright could speak to us from the screen' (p. 196). The film is artful, and often deliberately self-conscious in its artfulness, but any self-consciousness seems

designed to delight rather than encourage or even allow critical
distance or perspective.

## BBC/Time-Life, 1979

Another good way to shut down contradictory messages and debatable meanings is with institutional blandness. The BBC television
version directed by David Giles, with David Gwillim as Henry, was
not the result of a driving individual passion but rather part of a
larger project of producing all 37 plays for the series. The institutional
context proved a great leveller for many of the productions, and
*Henry V* especially feels like it is just ticking off a box marked 'done
that one'. The series aimed for accessibility and wide appeal, but especially in the early productions like *Henry V* it didn't set about to
achieve those goals by being particularly exciting and innovative, but
rather by cautiously settling for being mostly acceptable. Almost all
the lines are there, but that is no guarantee that much of interest gets
done with them. Certainly the modest budget, limited shooting time,
and most especially the intended display format – a 20ish-inch box
only a few feet from its viewer – take us back to the Chorus's apology
for 'In little room confining mighty men' (Epilogue, line 3), at least
compared with Olivier's expansive artistry. Actually, this particular
electronic 'little room' discourages men from being mighty. Unlike
the physical space of the Globe theatre, where an actor's vocal and
physical power can grab an audience, and judicious throttling back
of that power can reel them in, or on film, where close-ups can be
intense and long shots can handle big climaxes, on television when
actors shout or make strong gestures they often seem grotesque, and
when acting in close-up they can appear dangerously passive or diffi-
dent, and only ever just 'life-sized'.

Limited means can be a virtue, and perhaps the best part of this
version is its opening. The first Chorus speech is done in a single shot,
with Alec McCowen beginning as a talking head barking out of the
blackness behind him; gradually lights are brought up, and he
continues his speech while walking through a tableau of the English
court. The lights around the Chorus fade out again as he finishes, and

we seem to cut to a new location where Canterbury and Ely kneel to pray. Their sequence – whispered, fast, tense, and conspiratorial as they freeze when someone is heard to walk by – ends not with another cut and change of location but with the lights coming up to reveal where they have been all along. We are not in a church but in the same state room where the entire English court was arranged in that opening tableau. Henry is 'on hold' but already there on his throne, and Canterbury needs only take a few steps to get to his place before the King. The visual 'trick' is clever and its implication is striking: the clerics have been conspiring in full view, and the entire English court has been pretending not to notice them. The clerics step forward, the still court comes to life, and private vested interests merge seamlessly into the larger public debate. We might have been fooled about where we were in terms of location, but we know exactly where we are in *realpolitik* terms.

Unfortunately, the level of inventiveness and incisiveness drops off from there. The other members of the English court are given to much mumbled rhubarbing and bobble-headed 'active listening' during the rest of the scene, and the final physical action – Henry taking several tennis balls out of the Dauphin's gift box to toss around as he exits – descends into the sad spectacle of middle-aged and older nobles laughing too heartily while engaging each other in a manly game of catch. In this context, 'Now all the youth of England are on fire' becomes deeply unintentionally ironic, if such a thing were possible.

We get more coarse acting with the Eastcheap crew, performing like they were in a Benny Hill sketch satirizing Bad Shakespeare – at least in Olivier this was intentional, and it stopped after this scene. The conspirators are dispatched effectively, but the small scale makes Henry's tearful sense of betrayal more like soap opera (re)acting than profound grief at another 'fall of man'. The French court is set in a kind of blue boxing ring, suitable for its very raucous inhabitants. The end of Act II, scene iv, with Exeter's bombshell about Henry having already landed going off in an explosion of crowd reactions, leaves the poor French King ignominiously trying, and failing, to shout his final lines over what must be the French for 'rhubarb'.

The Harfleur material is bland, with the more ugly of Henry's threats cut, and we get more coarse acting from a Fluellen whose comic *shtick* begs for a response that no laugh track is there to provide. The language lesson, filmed at the beginning and again at the end with frosted edges to the frame, is interminable, like listening to a rendering of 'The Twelve Days of Christmas' that keeps starting over at the beginning when one hopes it might finally be done. The scene of the French camp the night before Agincourt shows how playing a scene where the only direction seems to be 'they are bored' very quickly just becomes boring to watch. Meanwhile, the sight of Fluellen crawling backwards through the English tents, under a blanket and with much shrubbery about his helmet, is at least second-rate Monty Python, but when Gower gets under the blanket with him we seem to have descended to *Carry On Camping*.

Gwillim's Henry seems of a piece with the production – understated, inoffensive, and not particularly forceful. The strongest character trait he exhibits appears to be 'ironic self-amusement' (Loehlin, p. 78). There is a light comedic, almost jokey energy to many of his big speeches and key moments, and the St Crispin speech most especially is delivered not heroically but with a mix of chumminess, irony and a few funny faces, like we're watching a Henry played by Hugh Laurie, or Hugh Grant. The production eschews judgement of Henry or his actions not through whitewashing cuts but through pedestrian choices and often noncommittal playing. The threats before Harfleur – edited, but not completely missing as in Olivier – don't seem to register; the argument with Williams is complete but without much initial impact and with only broadly comic consequences when resolved; and the line about killing the prisoners is spoken but nothing is done, no action is taken, and no one including Henry seems to react much to it at all. Even the problematic comparison of Henry and Alexander in Act IV, scene vii, simply passes under cover of the truly classic comic bit of Fluellen spitting bits of apple over poor Gower as he rambles on, eating and discoursing. The promotional blurb on the current DVD cover tells us that 'Henry V unites his people, invades France, deals with traitors, and cements the peace.' The production gives us this in more detail, but without much more urgency or depth.

## English Shakespeare Company, 1989

While the social context, explicit political stance, and many of the strong choices from this staging have been discussed in the previous section, the television version – filmed (mostly) live in performance in the final week of the three-year life of a production that had toured globally – offers a decent visual record of those choices. Going into the filming, director Michael Bogdanov was keenly aware of the shifting fortunes and impact of the production over its life span:

> I had mixed feelings about it all. On the one hand it was gratifying to think there would be a permanent record of the work, however fast it would be shot. On the other, so many moments from the original productions had been lost, so many performances had been changed, the acting was three years old, and I was mentally unprepared for it. (Bodganov and Pennington, *The ESC*, p. 218)

The entire *Wars of the Roses* cycle was ending its stage life in a run at the Grand Theatre, Swansea, and the filming was scheduled for the final performance of each play – twenty-one-plus hours of live theatre filmed in seven days. Bogdanov and his film crew worked with seven cameras, in fixed and mobile positions throughout the theatre, and from them recorded four live-mixed versions of the single performance. They had no studio, but were able to shoot some difficult episodes like fight sequences (and reshoot some of the bigger screw-ups) on the stage in the afternoon. The experience of capturing the performance was more like filming a live broadcast of a sports event than making a movie:

> It was maniacal. Despite familiarity with the shows (mine, not anyone else's) the moments came at me so fast, I was always one camera or one line behind. Or simply behind. Some famous close-ups missed: 'Once more unto the breach'. . . . An eighteen-hour day, briefings in the morning, pick-ups in the afternoon, paralysis setting in at 7:30; depression at roughly 10:45 pm.
> Shouting like a fool, swearing like a tr**per . . . 'Close up of Michael on 2 . . . missed it! Give me the 2 shot. Go wide! Go wide! On 6! Close-up of Andy on 4 – I mean 2 – I mean 3! ****! Missed it again! Take 6!' Take anything! Take me home, country road.   (p. 228)

For Bogdanov and company, the filming was just another in a long line of chaotic events that were remarkable simply for coming off at all.

Among casting changes from early in the production's life to its latter-day filming, two seem significant in regard not only to the quality of the individual performances but to their effect on the production as a whole. The first was brought about by the untimely death of John Price, Pistol in the original production and 1986/87 tour. Price brought a wild and anarchic energy to the part; he was mesmerizing in his audacity and crudeness, but had such a twinkle in his eye that I couldn't help but be pulled into his exploits, no matter what he was doing. He gave the 'low-life' so *much* life that, as a group, they were a seriously destabilizing force to any traditional reading of the play as Henry's story. The pull that Price exerted with the energized Eastcheap crew really made the production multi-vocal, as opposed to a relentless unfolding of events from Henry's perspective. Paul Brennen in the televised version is fine but not a lot more, and the entire production shifts back towards Henry as a result. The production still provides a critique of Henry, but without offering as much of a theatrical (if hardly moral) alternative. It's still okay for us not to like Henry, but he is really the only game in town.

The second major change involved the Chorus. For the *Henrys* tour and subsequently in the *Wars of the Roses* cycle, Falstaff in the *Henry IV* plays was doubled with the Chorus in *Henry V*. This casting manoeuvre, for audience members in for the long haul, added a touch of irony to the Chorus's proceedings. In John Woodvine's hands – the original Falstaff and Chorus – this irony of doubling developed into a subtle, questioning tone through all the Chorus's speeches. It was as if the Chorus, on stage throughout the show, was watching and telling us about an old friend who had taken a different path; his comments were not exactly objective but were made without judgement, as though he were always wondering if this was the best way for things, for Henry, to proceed. Neither condemning nor cheerleading, the effect was that of an open-eyed assessment of Henry and his story, but from someone who cared. Woodvine's replacement for the *Wars of the Roses* cycle and for the television version was Barry Stanton. Stanton just seems effusive, and his presence on the stage throughout is not recorded on camera throughout. Both the change in player and the shift in medium worked to remove a subtle but persistent question from the audience's minds, and the Chorus became an occasionally beautiful speechmaker, not really in the action and not part of its critique either.

Much of the performance as captured on video lacks the intensity, energy and scope of the live staging, but many memorable moments and distinctive choices still come through. The clerics here seem hardly conspiratorial but actually quite comfortable in what they're getting up to. That comfort level is taken into Act I, scene ii, where Henry's 'Sure, we thank you' (l. 8) to interrupt the Archbishop's praises is only slightly impatient, and Henry's subsequent warning that 'God forbid' the Archbishop should try to pull anything over on them is delivered in a tone and manner that suggests 'You know I have to say this.' The Archbishop shows no discomfort at the suggestion he could possibly be less than forthright; his physicality offers in reply 'Of course you have to say this, I *understand*.' It seems that 'much fall of blood' (l. 25) and making 'waste in brief mortality' (l. 28) are simply things to be taken in one's stride when running a powerful country. The playing throughout makes the scene neither grand and heroic nor dark and conspiratorial. With no one doubting the outcome, we move in a businesslike and efficient way from legal niceties right to the hostile takeover, with the shareholders voting with their hands as they applaud Henry after 'break it all to pieces' (l. 225).

The great *coup de théâtre* moments discussed earlier are here for us to see and appreciate, but some smaller moments also stand out. After 'Once more unto the breach' the Eastcheap Four huddle down, leaning against the sandbags Henry just leapt from (the tank never made it to the end of the run); after Fluellen drives them off to the front line, the Multinational Four take up exactly the same position. It's a nicely ironic visual because it links the two groups together, but not exactly in the kind of unity Henry was espousing. And if Pennington's Henry is not as prickly, disturbing and disturbed as he appeared earlier in the run, the performance is still compelling, and commendable for sticking to its anti-heroic guns.

This television version is perhaps best watched as part of the whole epic cycle, and perhaps best appreciated as part of the epic struggle Bogdanov and Pennington went through to make it all happen. The production may have become less radical over its run and by the point of its filming (Loehlin, pp. 123–7), but whether regarded as 'brilliant [and] glitter[ing] with bright ideas' (Rothwell , p. 120) or 'relentlessly cynical [and] a queasy triumph' (Smith, *Henry*, pp. 73–4), this *Henry V* is an invigorating and useful reappraisal of the play and of many of the received ideas that became attached to it. The performance allows for and encourages critique of Henry and his project, something Kenneth Branagh in his feature film offers with one gritty, realistic hand only to take back with the skilful (cinematic and emotional) manipulations of the other.

## Branagh, 1989

Kenneth Branagh's acting motto when creating the role for the stage in 1984 was 'Do not judge this man, place him in context – *understand!*' (*Players of Shakespeare 2*, p. 100). This is sound practice for an actor – you have to live in your character, in his actions, and you're going to have a tough time playing those actions if you yourself have already judged them. However, a director, especially a film director, has a lot of power and control over the entire story and so inevitably shapes the action, and guides (or manipulates) our emotional responses to it. Because Branagh the director has so much control over that context in which Branagh the actor places his Henry, it's a significant but simple step to go from understanding the character to putting the audience in his shoes – and making sure everybody watching likes him.

The film begins simply enough, with Derek Jacobi's Chorus walking through a soundstage filled with the trappings of a film set. The soundstage is deserted and silent, save for Jacobi's voice, until 'Pardon gentles all,' at which point the musical soundtrack kicks in, first softly but very soon quite insistently. Most of the recurring themes of the score are introduced here. The Chorus is making a play for our 'imaginary forces' to help out, and the overt soundtrack is helping our imaginations with emotionally coloured strains that are by turns heroic, passionate, and full of intrigue. The soundtrack builds, Jacobi gains momentum and forcefulness, and as he throws open a huge set of doors on the set, he shouts his last phrase: 'OUR PLAY!' But the doors open to blackness, and the soundtrack cuts out. In the blackness, another door opens a crack and quickly shuts again. The next shot takes us into a very dark room, with the conspiratorial clerics in close-up, whispering softly.

The contrast between the Chorus's stirring rhetoric, ably assisted by the score's heightened emotionalism, and the spare, understated, downbeat sequence of 'seasoned, worried politicians on their mettle' (Branagh, p. 17) that follows, perfectly captures the mixed signals of the opening of the play. Branagh then gives us an incredibly over-the-top entrance (with over-the-top musical accompaniment) for Henry, cloaked and silhouetted, seemingly through those same huge doors the Chorus opened at the end of his speech. It's as though this wonderfully over-inflated, Darth Vader-esque arrival of our hero is what the Chorus *wanted* to follow his bellow and flourish, except the damned *script* put another scene in the way. Branagh gives us an ironic visual/aural bait-and-switch with the Chorus to Clergy shift, while still linking the Chorus's exuberance to the (eventual) entrance of our hero. However, the next sequence of images better indicates the larger strategy. After his followers all bow to the camera-as-Henry as it passes, when we finally see Henry he is unprepossessing, very young and, with his fresh face and tousled hair, almost cute. This may be meant to undercut the grandiose entrance with a more human reality, but the effect of the contrast between the foreboding silhouette and the lad perched on the throne is not ironic but endearing. The big image gets undercut, but we are drawn closer to this 'real' Henry.

Branagh might give us a little discontinuity and contradiction, but by no means does he turn that to any critique of power or of Henry himself. Like the information-management strategy of embedding reporters with troops for wartime coverage, we as audience members for Branagh's film are taken so intensely and intimately into the action that we have no time or distance from which to judge it. It takes a conscious effort to stand apart from the compelling filmmaking and intensity of the viewing experience in order, not to be ungrateful, but to gain some perspective on the many things taken for granted to make the experience so powerful – when you are that thoroughly embedded in the action, you stop questioning how you got there.

That seems to be the story Branagh creates within the film in his treatment of the Chorus. The Chorus begins in a film studio, obviously distanced from realistic action, but then appears on location for the fleet's departure, huddled near the front lines as explosions go off at Harfleur, marching with the troops and then hanging around the camp on the eve of Agincourt, and finally walking through the front lines just before the battle begins. The Chorus is visually drafted into Henry's army and embedded in the fighting. It's no wonder – in fact, it seems a strategic choice – that he goes from shouting and throwing the doors open on the action at the beginning to closing those same doors quietly and slowly at the end, so as not to disturb the intimate tableau of marriage and reconciliation with the larger bad news his final speech contains.

The video or DVD of the film is so easy to get, and there are so many interviews, reviews, articles and books that deal with it, that I will not try to be exhaustive in my commentary here. Instead, I'll turn to two scenes where all these productions show their interpretive hands, giving special attention to Branagh's film. The death of Bardolph can have big implications for Henry. Is he uncaring or distraught? Do we see the public figure win out over the private man, the real person finally subsumed in the role? And what is the effect of killing off the supposed comic characters? At over 170 lines, the wooing of Catherine is the most extensive encounter between English and French in the play; Henry speaks more lines to her than he does answering the Dauphin, exhorting his troops back to the breach, threatening the Governor before Harfleur, and preparing his men's hearts for Agincourt, *all combined*. She is his 'capital demand' in a political settlement, but he says many times how much he loves her; she has no choice, but he really wants her to say 'yes'. So, is the scene about romance or rape? Is it a love-suit or the continuation of war by other means? Are we watching two attractive young people come together, or watching the cat play with the mouse? Is it coercion or consent?

## Direct Comparisons: Killing Bardolph, Wooing Catherine

Olivier cuts Bardolph's death completely. The film goes from the French King's 'Bring us word of England's fall' (III.v.68) right to Montjoy's arrival before the English with his message about ransom (III.vi.115). Both Bardolph and Nim simply disappear from the film, not casualties of war or of discipline but victims of cutting that seems designed to reduce the 'difficult' aspects of Henry's character and actions.

In the BBC version, at least the lines are there. When Fluellen speaks of 'one Bardolph, if your majesty know the man' (III.vi.103–4) we cut to a close-up of Henry, who suddenly tenses. Henry slowly speaks his response, and the gentle tone of the whole speech makes him into the 'gentler gamester' (ll. 113–14) of his occupying strategy. There is no conscious irony in Gwillim's playing or anyone's reactions about gentle gamesters ordering the execution of old friends. When Montjoy arrives, Gwillim's Henry recovers himself very quickly, turning his response into a deftly played comedic set-up for the punchline about his men being 'almost no better than so many French' (l. 146). Because the scene is played with little urgency or sense of the personal stakes involved for anyone, including the condemned man we don't see, the effect on Henry's character and his enterprise, to this viewer, seems minimal.

In the ESC version, Pennington's Henry is very excited about the news from the bridge, but those high spirits die away on the mention of Bardolph. At the end of Fluellen's speech, Bardolph is forcibly escorted across the upstage catwalk, from which he calls out 'My Lord!' to Henry down below before disappearing. Two shots are heard coming from off-camera. Henry's following speech comes across as a recognition that he is too far in now to let his personal feelings do anything more than register then retreat. As in the BBC version, Henry seems fully recovered in time to play mercilessly with Montjoy on his entrance. The treatment of Bardolph's death helps to confirm our belief that this Henry is one cool customer, committed to the path he has chosen.

Branagh makes the most of this episode in his version, and the scene he creates is gripping. During Fluellen's speech, Bardolph arrives on his death cart with Exeter as executioner hulking over him. We get a close-up of Bardolph, then one of Henry where he gives a slight nod to Exeter. After Exeter violently hauls Bardolph to his feet, we get an extraordinary sequence of lengthy, silent close-ups, from Henry, to Bardolph, to Henry, to Bardolph, to Henry, and then into an interpolated memory sequence from Henry's tavern days, where Bardolph's joke about Henry not hanging a thief when he is king is met by the young Hal's prescient 'No, thou shalt.' We get a close-up of Hal/Henry, then a close-up of Bardolph in the tavern that cross-fades to Bardolph in the noose, then a close-up of Henry where he signals for Exeter to finish the job. Branagh's voice threatens to crack on 'We would have all such offenders . . .' but he then continues very strongly, hiding his grief under a stern announcement to all his men. The grief comes back at the end, however, as his voice threatens to break again for the final line about the 'gentlest gamester'. Immediately following that line, we cut to a close-up of the dead Bardolph's face, with his eyes rolling back.

The breaking voice and the gruesome close-up seem to give the aural and visual lie to Henry's 'gentle gamester' line of argument. The entrance of Montjoy beneath the hanging man, uncomfortably glancing up at the corpse, seems further to drive the irony home. But the overall effect of the sequence is not to the disadvantage of Henry's character. Because of all the intense close-ups – including one where tears roll down Henry's cheek – and because unlike the other versions Henry does *not* recover quickly and in fact keeps his very dark mood right through to the end of the scene, the effect is to show the great cost to Henry of being the leader. Pistol, whose earlier pleading for his friend was almost unbearably painful to watch, only gets a very brief shot of his reaction to the death, as part of a larger crowd (compared with the many lengthy close-ups of Henry). Pistol's story is minimized further when we see a shot of the reaction of the men to Montjoy's speech, where Pistol, now on screen for a couple of seconds, gives a quizzical look to the Frenchman but apparently no more consideration to his hanging dead friend.

In the staging directions for this sequence in his screenplay, Branagh writes that 'the cost to the King is enormous' (p. 71), and in the Introduction he states 'the flashback during Bardolph's on-screen execution help[s] to illustrate the young king's intense isolation' (p. 12). The death of Bardolph is really all about Henry, but in a good way, one that deepens his character and encourages us to empathize with the difficulties and sacrifices that come with his office. The human content of Bardolph's story, and the disintegration of the Eastcheap band of brothers, is negated by Branagh's image-making as surely as it was by Olivier's cuts. Branagh's audacious move in bringing the execution of Bardolph into plain view and playing it out at excruciating length, actually has the effect of making us feel sorry for Henry, not for the man in the noose. Later on, we don't hear from the Boy (IV.iv.66) that Nim is hanged (presumably again on Henry's orders) because that speech is cut; instead we see Nim being stabbed in the back by a French soldier as he is pilfering the pockets of corpses at Agincourt. In both cases – the brilliantly staged and the textually altered – Henry's old friends die, but it's not his fault. When French women on the field run at the English King in Branagh's famous tracking shot through the desolation after Harfleur, it is Montjoy, a Frenchman, who holds them back; this may be a diplomatic gesture, but it also reads a bit like the loser saying of the winner 'It's okay, he's only done what he had to do.' Branagh goes still further with the images under Burgundy's speech in Act V, scene ii. We get a close-up of the French King and then a flashback image of the French dead, followed by a close-up of Henry and then a flashback montage of the English dead – York, the Boy, Quickly, Nim, Bardolph, Scrope and even Falstaff. The sequence is constructed as a visual list of all Henry has lost – lost, not killed or executed or led to their deaths. The sequence is designed to make us feel for Henry, but not to measure his culpability or the ideological underpinnings that make such things 'necessary'.

Olivier introduces the wooing scene with the funniest moment in the film. When Henry asks the French Queen 'Will you, fair sister, / Go with the princes . . .?' he very gently nods his head, 'Yes,' and when he follows with 'or stay here with us?' (V.ii.90–1) he very gently shakes his head, 'No.' His subtle powers of persuasion move Isobel off with the rest, and as they leave, an angelic choir comes in on the soundtrack to serenade the Princess and her Prince Charming in their story-book setting. The angelic voices only fade out when Henry compares Catherine herself to an angel. Renee Asherson's playing is all innocence, and she is almost always smiling at Henry. During his first long speech, she leans in towards him, looking for the compliment on 'To say to thee that I shall die, is true –' (ll. 149–50); when he finishes 'but for thy love, by the Lord, no,' she jumps away offended, and we get a reaction shot of Alice looking disappointed. Henry gets very close to her again by the end of that speech, at which point she walks away and gazes out of a window before delivering 'Is it possible dat I sould love de *ennemi* of France?' (l. 166). Her reaction is melancholy rather than angry. For his part, Henry laughs heartily at his little joke about loving France so well he 'will not part with a village of it' (ll. 169–70). Catherine is smiling at him again by the beginning of his bad French, and giggling by the end of it.

The one other melancholy moment comes as Catherine bows her head for 'Dat is as it shall please de *roi mon pere*' (l. 238). Again, it doesn't last, as Catherine is soon fluttering away from Henry's hand-kiss. On Henry's 'O, Kate, nice customs curtsy to great kings' (l. 260), the angelic choir returns, just in time for the kiss between the lovely innocent and the virile heartthrob. Catherine isn't very responsive physically, but she doesn't pull away either. No matter, because after the kiss we get a close-up of their clasped hands; the fleur-de-lis insignia is on her ring and the lion is on his, but their intertwining fingers unite the two symbols into a visual indicator of reconciliation and closure. The off-colour exchanges with Burgundy are cut, as are the lines where Henry says his wooing has been less than successful. Overall, the scene is charming and pretty, a medieval fairy-tale ending for a lush Technicolor romance.

The BBC version, not surprisingly after the soft focus and frosted-edges of the language lesson, plays the scene romantically as well. This version uses a lot of reaction shots of Jocelyne Boisseau's Catherine, to let us see how Henry is doing and guide our response. Early in Henry's first big speech, we get a reaction shot of blank looks from Catherine and Alice, as if they really don't understand him. Later there is a reaction shot where they look a bit more sympathetically at him. Still later, Henry gets a smile from Catherine when he talks of a 'good leg' (l. 157). Near the end of the speech there is a shot of her looking up at him with a face that says 'He's dreamy!' As in

Olivier, Catherine retreats from Henry for the 'ennemi of France' line. As in Olivier, Henry's bad French wins her, and Alice, back again, as the two women nod encouragement to him following every butchered line, and giggle at the end.

Catherine bursts out laughing at Henry's 'Can any of your neighbours tell, Kate? I'll ask them' (ll. 190–1). She tries to hide it, but Henry catches her out, and his 'Come, I know thou lovest me' sounds like a cross between 'Come out, come out, wherever you are' and 'Busted!' His request for her to 'put off [her] maiden blushes' (l. 226) seems only reasonable here, as Boisseau's playing comes off as mostly coy. When Henry kisses her, she continues to look up at him sweetly. As in Olivier, the Burgundy exchange and Henry's doubting lines are cut. While not exactly passionate, the playing certainly shows that Henry has won her over.

The wooing scene in the ESC version encourages critique of Henry's attitudes and actions rather than acquiescence to his charms. Out of Pennington's mouth, the request to 'leave our cousin Catherine here with us' (l. 95) sounds threatening, maybe not to her but certainly to the rest of the French court, who he has over a barrel. He sits far back at a table, she forward in a chair. This Henry is making small talk; he even gives a bored half-shrug when he asks 'Do you like me, Kate?' (ll. 106–7), as if his expectations are low indeed. His lines about her being like an angel are delivered in a swift monotone. But when Catherine all but calls him a liar, far from being angry Henry finally takes an interest; her spirited response draws him a bit closer to her, as if he's glad she called him on his glib bullshit. His 'clap hands and a bargain' (l. 130) seems an attempt to call a spade a spade, but this Catherine isn't calling it anything. In the many reaction shots of Francesca Ryan's Catherine through the scene, she tends to give nothing away. If anything, she seems a bit tense and to be wondering just what this man is doing. These guarded reaction shots allow us to maintain some objectivity about Henry's display, as well.

By the time he gets to the end of his long speech, this Henry has talked himself into being a bit smug about the opportunity he's offering her to 'take a king' (l. 164). He seems quite pleased with himself when he asks 'Speak, my fair' as he crosses his leg, taps his foot, and brushes some imaginary lint from his trouser-leg, all the while not even looking at her. His response to her question about loving France's enemy starts out condescending, then turns into an almost sneering joke about how much he loves France – which, in a reaction shot, this Catherine does not find amusing at all. Henry's bad French gets something like a grudging smile, but perhaps because she's enjoying watching him squirm for a moment. If so, he gets her back by finally moving very close to her and emphasising the comments about loving her 'cruelly' (l. 196) and about her future role as a 'good soldier-breeder' (l. 199) – unromantic lines both.

Catherine's lines about the match being up to her father, not her, seem in this playing to throw all Henry's tactics back in his face, or at least back into the arena of political settlements where we started. Henry keeps trying, and he gets his kiss, or rather takes it, his words 'patiently and yielding' (l. 266) in this context confirming power relations and again not very romantic. Again, in reaction shots through the latter part of the sequence, Catherine tends to be just looking at him, giving Henry and us nothing to indicate his progress or guide our reactions. She doesn't spit in his face, but she doesn't smile sweetly either. Even without the Burgundy exchanges (a strange cut, perhaps, given the staging choices) the sequence reads more as sly compelling of consent rather than delightful falling in love. With the clear-eyed non-response of Ryan, the great disparity of lines comes across as Catherine giving Henry enough rope to hang himself.

Branagh takes full advantage of his medium for carefully placed reaction shots, skilful camera work, an underlining score and carefully modulated vocal delivery. The fact that he was acting opposite his then-partner Emma Thompson added extra-filmic charm at the time. Henry's request for Catherine to be left with him is delivered firmly, but Branagh then uses his gentle voice for 'She is our capital demand . . .' (ll. 96–7) and the romantic score is brought in underneath, taking the edge off the political context and setting the stage for the romantic encounter to come. The scene starts formally, with the two of them at opposite ends of a long council table, but Branagh the director's use of close-ups and Branagh the actor's deft comic timing work against the distant/distrustful spatial relations. Branagh creates a very funny moment after Catherine's confession that she doesn't speak English, by inserting a long pause after 'O' (l. 104) and then bumbling sheepishly and awkwardly through the 'angels' compliment. Catherine's response doesn't deliver a stinging accusation of false flattery but rather a tone of 'O God, I'm dealing with a social moron.' Henry catches the tone, which makes him a bit petulant in dropping his efforts and asking for a handshake and to call it a day. The romance comes back for 'take a soldier, take a king' with the reappearance of the romantic music. Both the music and Henry's very gentle response take the sting out of the '*ennemi* of France' line, and Branagh delivers the potentially unattractive lines about how much he loves France in an uninflected fashion. This strategic playing leaves them both open for honest and appealing shared laughter through Henry's pathetic attempts at French and Catherine's reassurance that he's not so bad.

'Can any of your neighbours tell . . .' is delivered with brilliant comic timing, and gets a very pleased reaction shot from Alice – she looks on with a smile that shows her to be rooting for these two attractive and charming young things to get together. As the scene progresses, we get more smiles from Catherine, more of Branagh's breathy gentle voice, and more romantic music. In the medium shot when Catherine says the match is 'as it shall please de *roi mon pere*' she faces forward and drops her eyes, and Henry is in profile on the other side of the frame. On his whispered 'Nay, it will please him well . . .' he reaches out, gently takes her by the chin, and turns her head to face him, as if to say 'Don't think about politics, what do *you* want?' Catherine's retreat over kissing hands or lips is a momentary aberration, as she smiles again during Henry's 'O Kate . . .' response. Although the line is still spoken, there is no need here for Henry's 'patiently and yielding . . .' since the shot for the kiss shows both their faces moving symmetrically in profile towards the centre of the frame, blocking out the lions and fleur-de-lis on Burgundy's chair in the background as their lips come together. Similar to Olivier's clasped hands and signet rings, here the pretty young things in the foreground eclipse the symbols of France and England to provide a romantic image of union in the flesh. Having Catherine move in for the kiss with Henry implies another symmetry, one of mutual attraction and equal interest that 'corrects' the vast disparity in lines and huge power difference between conqueror and conquered. The happy ending is hard won after so much carnage, and the filming and playing of the scene leave no room to question that happiness.

Branagh was drawn to *Henry V* precisely because of the complexities, contradictions and ambiguities: 'The war seemed to be inevitable and regrettable and ugly and sad and exciting, intoxicating and seductive' (Nightingale). In Branagh the director's hands, playing the contradictions just makes Henry more interesting, and mixing human moments (tears, anger, bashful wooing) with the bloodlust makes him endearing rather than problematic. Still, it might be worth debating all the way to the pub whether Branagh's fine comic timing outweighs, hides or erases any problems we might have with Henry's agenda, or if even Pennington's prickly personification still wins us over, because (a) the action shows him to be effective, and (b) we don't have much of an alternative. After all, should we applaud the conspirators' assassination attempt, and would we really rather have, say, Pistol in charge? Is it really possible for us to like Henry and hate what he does, or for us to critique the action even through the hero who drives it? Does the play and its performances give us subversive elements well contained, or containment strategies well subverted? It's something like this last question that underlies much recent critical work on the play.

# 6 Critical Assessments

Like stage productions and screen adaptations, acts of critical engagement are a matter of making choices – of what seems most important, of what will serve as the inflected moments and/or elements for analysis, and so of what becomes foregrounded in an argument about what a play does. Like productions, critical works are also historically and culturally contingent, and no line of argument ever has the last word.

## Early Assessments of the Genre

One of the earliest responses to Shakespeare's plays glances at most of the elements for analysis that criticism has been engaging with ever since. In 1592, Thomas Nashe wrote to defend stage plays as 'a rare exercise of virtue' and the history play was his chosen exemplum:

> [T]he subject of them ... is borrowed out of our English Chronicles, wherein our forefathers' valiant acts (that have lain long buried in rusty brass and worm-eaten books) are revived, and they themselves raised from the Grave of Oblivion, and brought to plead their aged Honors in open presence: than which, what can be a sharper reproof to these dangerous effeminate days of ours? How would it have joyed brave Talbot (the terror of the French) to think that after he had lain two hundred years in his Tomb, he should triumph again on the Stage, and have his bones new embalmed with the tears of ten thousand spectators at least (at several times), who, in the Tragedian that represents his person, imagine they behold him fresh bleeding.

As an early piece of genre criticism, Nashe asserts that these history plays borrow from their historical sources but transform them and make the material better – more affecting and more immediate. That affect and immediacy is why performance critics situate the real life of the plays in the theatre rather than in their not-quite-worm-eaten book form. As a character study, Nashe's words attest to the kind of intense identification with a character that often drives such critical work. Nashe also raises complex social and political issues with which recent criticism has been wrestling. When Nashe alludes to the 'dangerous effeminate days of ours' he seems to espouse a rigid and gendered distinction between 'masculine' heroism and martial pursuits and 'feminine' weakness and idleness, which such history plays provide distraction from and reproof of. This casual sexism may be a criticism of the reigning female monarch, or a reflection of socialized anxiety regarding female rule. Certainly Nashe's politics, and his understanding of the theatre's function, are conservative. He thinks of plays as 'bones to gnaw upon, which may keep [the lower classes] from having leisure to intermeddle with higher matters', and later says that, without plays to distract him, a ne'er-do-well would otherwise be 'devising upon felony or treason, and how he may best exalt himself by mischief'. Nashe makes it sound as if one of the things standing between an ordered nation and anarchy is a distract-ing theatre that also uncomplicatedly shows virtue rewarded and vice punished.

The theatre seems like a convenient mechanism for maintaining obedience to the state, but the specific play Nashe uses reveals a fault-line running through this notion. The audience isn't cheering Talbot on in blind jingoistic patriotism but weeping for his death. Talbot goes to his death because his own side sold him out; in *Henry VI, Part 1* he is referred to as the 'bought and sold Lord Talbot' (IV.iv.13), and it is 'the fraud of England, not the force of France, / Hath now entrapped [him]' (ll. 36–7). Such 'valiant acts' and 'aged honors' as Nashe so commends are shown to be wasted by poor leadership, a dissentious and self-interested aristocracy, bad faith, etc. Nashe is silent on why a crowd worked to emotional outbursts by this hard historical truth is then unable to consider the ignoble and 'effemi-nate' (V.vi.107) situation of the play in terms of the 'dangerous effem-inate days of ours' Nashe says the play precisely functions to rebuke. In light of what Shakespeare's play actually stages of Talbot's demise, what is the contemporary subject of its 'sharp reproof' – the idle audience? The French? Weak monarchs? Foreign quarrels? The cynical use-value of heroism to those in power? Of continuing concern is whether a play is a social distraction, neatly containing any responses within the safe fictions of an essentially conservative artform, or if its representations of history (intentionally or unavoidably) interrogate past actions and contemporary issues for any to see and reprove, in their own way, if they so choose.

Francis Meres, in his *Palladis Tamia* of 1598, praises Shakespeare as the most excellent English writer for comedies and tragedies. It's not that Meres didn't think the histories were any good – it's just that he listed them under 'Tragedies'. The First Folio of 1623 gives these plays that 'borrow' their subject matter from the *Chronicles* their own generic title of 'Histories'. Emma Smith, in introductory materials to the collection of criticism in *Shakespeare's Histories* (2004), provides an excellent survey (from which the rest of this paragraph is drawn) of early responses to the genre at the hands of critics, editors and theatrical adapters. Many early commentators, along with complaining about Shakespeare's neglect of the Classical unities, seemed to revert to Meres, trying to move the hybrid genre back towards either comedy or tragedy through analysis or adaptation. Others, like Samuel Johnson writing in the 1760s, felt that the histories made the political into the personal, and so should be read as character studies. Even while the Romantics were focused on Shakespeare's fine and varied characterizations (although Hazlitt famously found Henry V to be a 'very amiable monster'), other ideas were being expressed. Schlegel saw the histories as forming one great whole, and Coleridge put forth the argument that plays about England written for an English audience must *ipso facto* be patriotic. By the late 1800s, the notion of Shakespeare's patriotic history was taken by Gervinus and Dowden to imply both a conservative political stance, where subjects must learn obedience, and a clear moral view, where bad deeds face inevitable retribution; it was also seen by Swinburne as providing, in *Henry V* specifically, a prototypical patriotic epic and imperialist hero well-suited to current days of Victoria and Empire.

It is not that critical assessment of the history plays neatly went from genre to character to something like political, and it's not that the only criticism really worth talking about was written from the mid-twentieth century on, but for the sake of space I want to focus on more recent critical debates, and for that, to start with Tillyard.

## Tillyard, Old/New World Order, Serial Thinking

For E. M. W. Tillyard, in *Shakespeare's History Plays* (1944), there are the plots and specific incidents that each of the plays relate, and then there is the bigger story that lies behind them all – in fact, that gets told by the sequence of histories when considered as a 'whole contemporary pattern of culture' (p. 3). On the level of plot and incident, 'the picture we get from Shakespeare's Histories is that of disorder' (p. 7), but in the larger picture, 'when Shakespeare deals with the concrete facts of English history he never forgets the principle of order behind all the terrible manifestations of disorder' (p. 17). Tillyard lays out a value-system for Shakespeare's time that encompasses history and politics, individual action and national pursuits, heaven and earth, all in 'a unity, in which everything had its place' (p. 11). This Elizabethan World Order is imagined as a ladder or a chain, and harmony is maintained in part through adherence to the hierarchy – everything and everyone staying in their appropriate place. Working together with this worldview is a contemporary political view, the Tudor Myth, that sees 'the union of the two houses of York and Lancaster' – and all the monarchs since Henry VII – representing 'the providential and happy ending of an organic piece of history' (p. 29). Shakespeare's history plays then function as a larger unit(y), bringing to the theatre the 'moral drama' (p. 42) from the Chronicles for a 'total sequence' that 'expressed successfully a universally held and still comprehensible scheme of history: a scheme fundamentally religious, by which events evolve under a law of justice and under the ruling of God's Providence, and of which Elizabeth's England was the acknowledged outcome' (pp. 320–1).

Critics ever since have argued that such notions essentialize (and therefore leave out) a lot of social history, and a lot of what's in the plays. Tillyard sees the plays as political, as have many critics since, but the politics is conservative, even reactionary: 'behind the unfolding of civil war there is the great lesson (implied always and rarely stated) that the present time must take warning from the past and utterly renounce all civil dissension' (p. 155). I'm not sure anyone would argue that civil war is good, but Tillyard's equation of past civil war with contemporary civil dissension makes it inconceivable that Shakespeare may have started from the moral chronicles but dramatically questioned 'what price order?' or 'is this the way power should work?' or 'how should we be governed?' For Tillyard, the plays are answers, not questions.

Tillyard's overarching arguments give him some problems in his analysis of *Henry V*. He suggests that Shakespeare treated the play as something of a contractual obligation in completing the sequence: 'having achieved popularity in showing Henry's youthful dissipation he could not, without scandal, refuse to show Henry in his traditional part of perfect king'. But 'in creating his epic of England Shakespeare had set himself an exacting standard. His political hero, to be worthy of the standard just set, must be the symbol of some great political principle. And there was no principle he could symbolize' (p. 305). The character of Hal from the *Henry IV* plays, with his 'fundamental detachment and persistent irony', would not serve:

> Shakespeare came to terms with this hopeless situation by jettisoning the character he had created and substituting one which, though lacking all consistency, satisfied the requirements of both the chroniclers and of popular tradition. No wonder if the play constructed round him shows a falling off in quality.   (p. 306)

This hero king, set up in the great sequence as the exact opposite of the demon king Richard III, could not possibly be himself ironic, detached and unprincipled – even though Tillyard describes Henry in terms that could equally apply to Richard, as a 'man who knew exactly what he wanted and went for it with utter singleness of heart' (p. 313). These things could not possibly be the point of the play. It had to be about victorious acts, the story required a hero, he had to be 'good', so better to talk about Henry's 'pedestrian thoughtfulness' or hollow and 'detached eloquence', and a 'weak construction' and lack of 'intensity' and 'warmth', as 'the play's shortcomings' rather than Shakespeare's particular take on the material. For Tillyard, then, the overall pattern of moral drama has to work, even if the play itself doesn't.

Other critics also took a providential line in analysing the whole sequence and its relation to Shakespeare's times, while some tried to get politics back out of the equation again, focusing instead on Shakespeare's higher literary artistry and universal grasp of human nature. But in the twentieth century, it would be difficult to make political considerations of the past or the present disappear. If Tillyard in part wrote about Elizabethan history plays and politics to reassure himself during the Second World War, Polish theatre director Jan Kott in part wrote about the same material to express a despair about post-war totalitarianism. In Kott's *Shakespeare our Contemporary* (1964), the history plays were imagined as a vicious and destructive cycle rather than a linear progress towards order and a happy ending. History was still deterministic, just not the working out of God's providence but instead the repetitions of an indifferent 'Grand Mechanism' churning out new tyrants, new challengers, and new victims for historical tragedy. From this perspective, it is easy to see the Epilogue to *Henry V* not as an encomium to the high points but as the precipice at the top of Kott's 'grand staircase of history' – there is nowhere to go but down, and really, that's where we've been going all along.

The notion of grand patterns, whether seen optimistically or pessimistically, clearly sets the history plays up as a single, pre-planned entity, a huge symphony divided into movements with recurring national and political themes. Some more recent criticism questions that tight unity – after all, even Tillyard had no good reason why Shakespeare wrote the chronologically second tetralogy first, and had trouble with *Henry V* as Shakespeare's last word on the subject. Alexander Leggatt, in *Shakespeare's Political Drama* (1988), looks at each play 'as a fresh experiment' in 'a series of explorations of differing material, asking the same questions but not always getting the same answers' (pp. x–xi). Such a stance allows Leggatt to look thoroughly and sensibly, in the case of *Henry V*, at the play Shakespeare wrote instead of the one he should have written. The play comes across as challenging and highly exploratory, where 'we are not so much following an action as looking all around a subject, often in a discontinuous way. This includes not only characters and events but attitudes toward them, even ways of dramatizing them' (p. 114). Tillyard's 'shortcomings' are now the dramatic point, including the hot and cold characterization of Henry in his many performances through the play, as well as the contradictions and risky connections Shakespeare makes by way of critique in structuring the action.

In *Shakespeare's Serial History Plays* (2002), Nicholas Grene similarly argues for a view of the second tetralogy as an 'incremental series' rather than a done-deal from the outset, with Shakespeare as a writer 'never content to repeat himself, producing as a result a series that is chronologically continuous but formally discontinuous' (p. 247). This leads Grene into a character analysis not unlike Tillyard's, where Henry is simply not the same character as Hal from the *Henry IV* plays. Grene tests ironic readings and performances of the play – ones where 'gaps and interstices in [Henry's] shifting sequence of roles' (p. 243) are seen as intentional on Shakespeare's part – but finds them unconvincing precisely because of the lack of coherent characterization or clear identity for Henry. Unsustainable through-readings are undone, but only in a strange endgame of a discontinuous character, a discontinuous style, and a discontinuous play.

## Ambivalence and Ambiguity

A. P. Rossiter looked at the histories and saw double. In 'Ambivalence: the Dialectic of the Histories' (1951; in Rossiter, 1961), Rossiter suggests that,

> Looked at *one* way, the Histories present a triumphal march of the destinies of England. But look at them another way – at the individual lives of men and women – and your conclusion will be nearer to what Yeats wrote [of Shakespeare's histories]: 'He meditated . . . upon blind ambitions, untoward accidents, and capricious passions; and the world was almost as empty in his eyes as it must be in the eyes of God.'  (p. 41)

The pessimism of the Yeats quote also finds reflection in Kott's dark view of the plays, but Rossiter doesn't replace the one with the other as Kott does. Rossiter argues for Shakespeare's essential ambivalence, where 'two opposed value-judgments are subsumed . . . both are valid . . . [and] the whole is only fully experienced when both opposites are held and included in a "two-eyed" view' (p. 51).

Ambiguity and dramatic irony become essential elements of Shakespeare's histories, where characters, actions and ideals are constantly undercut, and where the universe is a tragi-comic one where the comic is used to expose doubts about serious endeavours:

> The Tudor myth system of Order, Degree, etc. was too rigid, too black-and-white, too doctrinaire and narrowly moral for Shakespeare's mind: it falsified his fuller experience of men. Consequently, while employing it as a Frame, he had to undermine it, to qualify it with equivocations: to vex its applications with sly or subtle ambiguities: to cast doubt on its ultimate human validity, even in situations where its principles seemed most completely applicable.     (p. 59)

The ambivalence, the 'doubleness', the two-eyed view, produce plays that are effective precisely because they are unstable; the dialectics of order and disorder, tragic and comic, create a theatrical world 'which recognizes the coextancy and juxtaposition of opposites, without submitting to urges . . . to obliterate or annihilate the one in the theoretical interests of the other' (p. 62). Strangely, as was the case for Tillyard, the history play Rossiter doesn't wholly apply his insights to is *Henry V*, as he found it more of a 'propaganda-play on National Unity: heavily orchestrated for the brass'. But he does believe that all the impressive rhetoric in the play 'shows how something is being stifled' in creating a rather 'one-eyed' king and character (pp. 57–8), and he would definitely *not* count himself among those who 'have difficulty in refusing the critics' directions to see Henry V as Shakespeare's ideal' (p. 63).

Rossiter also wrote most persuasively about the so-called Problem Plays, which he felt 'throw opposed or contrary views into the mind: only to leave the resulting equations without any settled or soothing solutions' (p. 128). Norman Rabkin, in 'Either/Or: Responding to *Henry V*' (1981), picks up and runs with both the point and the label for his analysis. Rabkin notes that the play's critics have often divided into two camps: those who see an ideal monarch displaying military virtues in an historical pageant, and those who see a ruthless, hypocritical Machiavel inhabiting a biting satire. Some have attempted to reconcile these two opposing positions, by saying that the 'real' meaning of the play lies somewhere in between, or that the dramatist just couldn't make up his mind, or that the play is ironic because the author didn't believe what he was saying and so took every opportunity to undercut it. Rabkin says that all these attempts are misguided, and argues that 'in *Henry V* Shakespeare created a play whose ultimate power is precisely the fact that it points in two opposite directions, virtually daring us to choose one of the two opposed interpretations it requires of us' (p. 34). Shakespeare's play, for Rabkin, is the equivalent of the gestaltist's line drawing of a rabbit/duck. The drawing forms a rabbit, and it forms a duck; both are there, both are 'real', and we can see both but never at the same time.

Rabkin hypothesizes that the problems raised in each of the earlier plays in the tetralogy had become so complex that an audience at the time would not have been able to predict how they could possibly be resolved. *Richard II* sets up an essential problem for all the plays: can one person satisfactorily combine 'manipulative qualities' essential for political success with spiritual qualities necessary to be fully human and accessible to the audience – is it possible to have 'a public man who is privately whole'? Rabkin argues that *Henry IV, Part 1* seems to suggest the answer is 'yes' while *Henry IV, Part 2* says 'no' and we have been deceived. Rabkin feels that *Henry V* doesn't resolve that dichotomy but continues it in a single play, where the audience is not sure what to think.

If *Henry V* is an extension of *Henry IV, Part 1*, then we are watching a tale of military exploits that give way to a comic ending in marriage. The play contains overwhelming, inspiring rhetoric, and a character who meets challenges, succeeds, is effective, and who is capable of public display and deep inwardness. If *Henry V* is an extension of *Henry IV, Part 2*, then we have no happy ending, as the last Chorus points out, and no 'good cause' for the war, as Williams believes. The reasoning behind the war becomes suspect, the battle of Agincourt inglorious and anticlimactic, and Henry's rhetoric violent and coercive.

Rabkin concludes that there is no compromise between these two

opposed camps of interpretation. We can't 'solve' the conflict
because this problematic play is about that conflict:

> The terrible fact about *Henry V* is that Shakespeare seems equally tempted
> by both its rival gestalts. And he forces us, as we experience and reexperi-
> ence and reflect on the play, as we encounter it in performances which
> inevitably lean in one direction or the other, to share his conflict.

The play shows us the conflict between our own private and public
selves, our longing for and distrust of authority, and 'the simultane-
ity of our own hopes and fears about the world of political action'
wrapped up in 'the inscrutability of history' (p. 62). For Rabkin, the
play isn't a falling-off or a dead end – it just leaves us with a lot of
work on our hands.


## Politics, Ideology, Power, Dissent

Once any all-encompassing view of the plays as benign delivery
devices for ideas of order and obedience gets shot through with
doubts and ambiguities, *Henry V* and the other history plays become
sites where political actions and structures, and the ideologies that
drive and support them, are contested rather than uncomplicatedly
affirmed. It is with this view that New Historicist, Cultural Materialist
and Feminist critical practices have opened up the plays in invigorating and provocative ways. Some of these assessments have been
almost as pessimistic as Kott's, while others, in showing how power
and ideology are constructs rather than givens, allow for dissenting
voices in Shakespeare's work and a more engaged critical voice in
their own.

Stephen Greenblatt's *Shakespearean Negotiations* (1988), which
includes his famous essay on *Henry V*, 'Invisible Bullets', identifies a
'social energy' encoded in the plays, circulated through the stories,
social practices, power relations and cultural fantasies that were
represented, contested and renegotiated for a playhouse audience.
Looking into *Henry V*, Greenblatt was specifically interested in
charisma – the 'compelling glamour of power' – and its potential
subversion. What he found was a play that 'deftly registers every

nuance of royal hypocrisy, ruthlessness, and bad faith – testing, in effect, the proposition that successful rule depends not upon sacred-ness but upon demonic violence – but does so in the context of a celebration, a collective panegyric to . . . the charismatic leader' (p. 56). There is something of both Rossiter's and Rabkin's double vision in this, but for Greenblatt it is clear which side wins out. The fact that Shakespeare records hypocrisy, ruthlessness and bad faith is what makes Henry interesting in the theatre, and 'the subversive doubts the play continually awakens originate paradoxically in an effort to intensify the power of the king and his war'. The effect of Henry's power is clear in the play, but the effect of the doubts is 'deferred':

> Deferred until after Essex's campaign in Ireland, after Elizabeth's reign, after the monarchy itself as a significant political institution. Deferred even today, for in the wake of full-scale ironic readings and at a time when it no longer seems to matter very much, it is not at all clear that *Henry V* can be successfully performed as subversive.   (pp. 62–3)

There are plenty of doubts, paradoxes and ambiguities in Henry's story as Shakespeare tells it, but they are produced as a part of Henry's exercise of power, not as something independent and capa-ble therefore of undermining it – either then, for Shakespeare's audi-ence, or now for us. We continue to 'piece out' imperfections, not despite but because of our recognition of doubts, rather than work to bring it all down.

Greenblatt's assessment could serve as an exact explanation of the power of Kenneth Branagh's film, which recuperates the 'difficult' bits of the action to draw us even closer to the man we somehow don't hold responsible for them. Joel Altman (1991) develops Greenblatt's main point further into theatrical effect and audience complicity, arguing that 'Shakespeare taps his audience's emotions and directs their understanding in such a way that they can admire the King and nurture hostile feelings toward him but also transfer those feelings, in solidarity with him, to the foreign enemy' (p. 3, n.). The play does not critique but rather generates 'aggressive emotions stirred by action and eloquence' (p. 3). The killing of the prisoners becomes a pleasure and release for the audience. Our implication and participation in the violence is then immediately expiated in displaced responsibility (the French deserved it for killing the boys, God fought for the English), communal triumph (with so few English dead), and gestures of reconciliation (with Williams, Fluellen, later the French nobility, and especially Catherine).

These arguments are not quite the same as saying that bad faith wins the day and we like it, nor are they as despairing as Kott, but they both seem to argue for the political and theatrical containment of the possibility for social change in history, its representations, and its audiences. Alison Thorne (2002) makes similar points, but believes that the play at least invites 'scrutiny of the rhetorical uses of history ascribed to the genre, by showing how the past is deployed to manipulate audiences (both on- and offstage) into identifying with a political enterprise founded upon a value system and material interests that must, in many cases, have been fundamentally at odds with their own'. She goes on to argue for a 'more complex, more divided affective response' than the Chorus – or Greenblatt and Altman – would seem to require. Rather than being so thoroughly effective at recuperating serious doubts, there is something precarious about a play that so 'vividly discloses the extent to which the monarchy's imperialistic exercise in nation-building depends upon the active collaboration of the common populace – in the context not only of the dramatic fiction itself but of the theatre in which that fiction was staged and consumed' (pp. 164–5). The audience is still implicated in a story that requires its complicity in the telling, but not every audience member has to react to the rhetoric of war and victory and nation-building in the same way. Being manipulated but being aware of being manipulated is at least a first step in making ideology visible; if we are aware we are saying 'yes' we may at least come to understand the possibility of saying 'no'.

Greenblatt famously, and somewhat enigmatically, ends 'Invisible Bullets' by saying 'there is subversion, no end of subversion, only not for us'. Because in a sense undeniably true – *Henry V* is performed, serious doubts are raised about the uses of power, but we stay and watch the show, and the revolution does not take place – Cultural Materialist and Feminist critics shift the terms of the debate to look for the possibilities and voices of dissent rather than wholesale subversion in the play. Who else can we listen to, if not just Henry and the Chorus, and what else can we hear, if not just the nationalist necessities of aggression?

Alan Sinfield's *Faultlines* (1992), which includes the much-anthologized essay 'History and Ideology, Masculinity and Miscegenation: the Instance of *Henry V*' (written with Jonathan Dollimore), lays out strategies of reading for dissent, in an illuminating and engaging fashion. To get out of the subversion/containment dilemma, Sinfield defines dissidence as 'refusal of an aspect of the dominant, without prejudging an outcome'. Power relations are not monolithic but two-way, and 'even a text that aspires to contain a subordinate perspective must first bring it into visibility; even to misrepresent, one must present. And once that has happened, there is no guarantee that the subordinate will stay safely in its prescribed place' (pp. 47–9). A pre-existing script for the theatre, and especially one based on historical events, will always be heavily culturally prescribed; Henry will always go to war, win at Agincourt, and get the girl in the end; the system is the system, and theatre keeps in its place. But if neither Shakespeare nor his actors can 'jump out of ideology . . . they do have a distinctive power – an ideological power – to write some of the scripts' (p. 26), and audiences 'do not have to respect closures' and 'can insist on our sense that the middle of [a play] arouses expectations that exceed the closure' (p. 48). There is the story, and then there are faultline stories running through it that we may follow if we wish.

Sinfield's dissident reading strategies aim to get past the essentialist unity of Tillyard and its pessimistic inversion in Kott, as well as the equally essentializing desire to find coherence and consistency in fictional characters (or in life). Instead, human beings and history itself are understood 'in terms of social and political processes' (p. 113). We then see choices rather than determinism, subordinate as well as dominant cultures, and the workings of ideology rather than things as they are.

Ideology often works to create the impression of a unified society. *Henry V* stages that process in Henry's rhetorical strategies uniting his men at Harfleur and again at Agincourt, and uniting French and English at the end. But the play leaves in that which should be effaced for total effectiveness: those who won't go to the breach; the warring captains on the English side; Williams's powerful arguments; Henry's night-time comment about the fools and wretched slaves of vacant mind and gross brain, which contradicts his social levelling; Pistol's final scapegoating and exclusion; the glaring lack of Catherine's consent. Like Greenblatt, Sinfield sees power drawn to and consolidated in the figure of the King, but 'even as [ideology] consolidates, it betrays inherent instability' (p. 114). The play then 'circles obsessively around the inseparable issues of unity and division, inclusion and exclusion' (p. 119), and Henry fails to hold it all together:

> The king finally has difficulty, on the eve of Agincourt, in sustaining the responsibility that seems to belong with the ideological power that he has engrossed to himself; thus the fantasy of establishing ideological unity in the sole figure of the monarch arrives at an impasse it can handle only with difficulty.

Instead of containing past and contemporary historical concerns in the irresistible charisma of its central figure, the play reveals 'not only the rulers' strategies of power, but also the anxieties informing both them and their ideological representation' (pp. 126–7). As interested, even implicated spectators to these mighty enterprises and their faultlines, we don't necessarily have to rush unto every breach with Henry to shore up gaps and resolve contradictions; any structural flaws are part of the show.

For a feminist critical practice, it would seem that *Henry V* is a man's, man's, man's, man's world, but Sinfield's interest in voices other than the dominant leads him to find faultlines in the play's coercive construction of aggressive masculinity, and the potential for a dissident version of the wooing scene. The play charts an almost hysterical fear of 'effeminacy' that drives the aggression and violence among men. This threatens to render the Salic Law speech incoherent not because of its length or historical detail but because it cannot speak the female from whom Henry claims succession – his great-great-grandmother Isabella – and instead masks the actual point by following up with continued reference to bloody, martial, victorious male ancestors. With the threats of rape at Harfleur and elsewhere, the acknowledgement of the wives and mothers who lose husbands and sons, and the forced submission of Catherine, the play reveals the cost to women of Henry's endeavours and male 'proof' of manhood. But Sinfield also finds room in the theatre for Catherine to resist its larger movements. In the wooing, Henry says much, Catherine says little, but she does *not* say the one word Henry extends the scene on and on just to hear: 'Yes.' Catherine 'may be seen as avoiding collusion with Henry's approaches through a minimalist strategy of one-line replies' as well as declining 'to join in the pretense that her preferences matter' (p. 138). In performance, we might see Henry, with all his lines and all his power, getting the girl but not exactly getting his way, in finally having to take what she will not give. He can bully her and force her, but since he needs her, in the end he takes what he can get; the masculine construct of victory through warfare and securing of victory through marriage is not immune to insecurities and contradictions, as we watch the hero struggle.

Valerie Traub (1992) is less sure than Sinfield about Catherine's theatrical agency or the efficacy of her voice in the scene. For Traub, Catherine's 'predicament is structural; whatever her individual power, it is subsumed by her ideological, political and economic function in the systematic exchange of women between men' (p. 63). Catherine may be a dead end for dissent, if her use-value to the patriarchy that calls the shots is so overdetermined.

In *Engendering a Nation* (1997), Jean Howard and Phyllis Rackin offer a committed social exploration of the history plays' constructions of meanings and a broader look at gender issues. Like Sinfield, they see 'not only masculinity but nationality and military prowess . . . now grounded in embodied sexual difference'. The 'performative masculinity' displayed throughout *Henry V* seems to necessitate the 'identification of rape as a model of male dominance' (p. 196). The action of the play, the accumulation of Henry's victories, tells a particularly vivid parallel story: 'the images of rape that characterize Henry's acquisition of a wife' – and, more broadly, his acquisition of France – 'establish, almost at the moment of its conception, the connection between the nascent bourgeois ideal of heterosexual marriage and the savage fantasies of rape that attend it' (p. 215). The play gestures at those who pay the cost, and how, for all Henry gains.

I'm not sure this is as pessimistic as Kott, but it may take us back to the realm of historical tragedy. At least Sinfield's work allows for the possibility of some (ideological and theatrical) play within the play, from a feminist and materialist standpoint. So too does Rackin's earlier work, in *Stages of History* (1990). Here Rackin charts the battle in a transition between opposing views of history, where 'explanations of events in terms of their first cause in divine providence were giving way to Machiavellian analyses of second causes – the effects of political situations and the impact of human will and capabilities' (p. 6). Shakespeare's history plays are an 'experimental' genre, where 'contradictory notions of historical truth and changing conceptions of historiography inform those experiments' (p. 27), as do oppositional histories and voices that 'official' history might like to suppress but that the 'volatile theatrical setting' (p. xi) for history plays could restore. The plays are, then, less monolithic and suppressive/oppressive in ideological determination or theatrical effect. They throw decisions about truth back into our court, as 'they cast their audiences in the roles of historians, viewing the events from a variety of perspectives, struggling to make sense of conflicting reports and evidence, and uncomfortably reminded of the anachronistic distance that separated them from the objects of their nostalgic yearning' (p. 28).

## Performance

Performance criticism can be informed by any of the committed viewpoints explored above, but it studies a play's effects primarily through actual performances, whether in extended reviews, stage histories, first-hand accounts of creating productions, or in conjunction with rigorous theoretical arguments about what constitutes the performative.

Of overviews of productions, Ralph Berry charts the *Changing Styles in Shakespeare* (1981) with a chapter on the play. More recently, Emma Smith's volume on *King Henry V* (2002) provides a detailed stage history in a thorough introduction, and then in documenting specific production choices cued line-by-line to the text. James Loehlin's volume on the play (1996) provides a brief pre-twentieth-century stage history, thorough and insightful analyses of six different twentieth-century productions, and an account of some productions outside the UK.

For specific productions, Pauline Kiernan's *Staging Shakespeare at the New Globe* (1999) offers valuable information about creative process and performance discoveries for the production of the play that opened the reconstructed Globe in London in 1997. Director Michael Bogdanov and actor Michael Pennington's book *The English Shakespeare Company* (1990) charts the birth and life of their *Wars of the Roses* cycle from 1986 to 1989, in a highly readable, warts-and-all manner. Vivid actor accounts of playing Henry can also be found in *Players of Shakespeare* 2 (Kenneth Branagh in 1984) and 6 (Adrian Lester in 2003).

Sophisticated theoretical work with texts, productions and reception can be found in Barbara Hodgdon's excellent *The End Crowns All: Closure and Contradiction in Shakespeare's History* (1991), with a chapter on how *Henry V*'s overdetermined ending gets reinforced or undone in various performances. Although only dealing with *Henry V* in passing, W. B. Worthen's *Shakespeare and the Force of Modern Performance* is a rigorous and provocative study of texts and performativity, taking into special account the new Globe and its effects.

I've not provided a lot of detail about performance criticism, primarily because the core of this book deals with performativity and reception. But I would like to end with some insights not from more critics but from other playwrights. I spent a lot of time in the Commentary section not just on what actors might do at particular moments of the playtexts, but also on various ways we might be responding to the unfolding events and the particular ways in which Shakespeare unfolds them. Similarly, I feel the best critical assessments of the play are ones that implicate the audience, implicate us, in the play's ideals, cynicism, violence, bad faith, brotherhood, compelling ideologies and tentative dissent. Perhaps more than any other play by Shakespeare, *Henry V* is about its audience – a test, even, but without direct questions or any kind of scoresheet. The challenges of *Henry V* require a particular way of being a theatre audience, and it is asking a lot. After all, not many of us would say we go to the theatre to struggle. British playwright Howard Barker (1993) has always tried to write the kind of play that 'expects no unity of response but encourages division, and restores responsibility to the audience' (p. 39) – his theatre company is appropriately called The Wrestling School. *Henry V*, as a fictional account of historical facts, as a play filled with contradictions, is a play that expects our dissatisfaction, and forces us to wrestle with whatever truth it may be telling. American playwright Tony Kushner (2004) reminds us that the truth is hard work:

> Truth is dialectical, by which I mean contradictory. Truth is fluid, not simple. Truth is not immutable, eternal or ahistorical. It changes in time. The ability to find truth has some proportional relationship to the struggle to find it and the vigor and rigorousness with which it is interrogated once found. I think it's salutary to ask yourself, over and over, if what you believe is true or just expedient, true or just comfortable or worse, just profitable? Truth is never finally entirely graspable, but neither is it entirely unknowable; glimpses of it come to the courageous, the curious, the diligent, the kind-hearted, the generous.

Because it provides an opportunity to struggle openly with some of our most difficult and important truths, *Henry V* remains vital, compelling and exciting theatre.

# Further Reading

For *Henry V*, there is further reading, no end of further reading, and especially for us. The last 25 years or so have seen notably prolific output, with new editions, an explosion of historically and theoretically informed critical work, more available information about stage productions that doesn't require trips to specialized archives, and much writing on cinematic versions. What follows in this section is certainly partial, and somewhat biased in terms of what I personally find to be informative, provocative and actually enjoyable to read.

## 1 The Texts and Early Performances

### Texts

Oxford: ed. Gary Taylor (Oxford: Oxford University Press, 1982). Based on F, but some interesting use made of Q; excellent introduction, plus sections of Holinshed in appendix.

New Cambridge: ed. Andrew Gurr (Cambridge: Cambridge University Press, 1992). Another superb and detailed introduction, plus appendices dealing with source material.

Arden: ed. T. W. Craik (London: Routledge, 1995). Appendix contains a complete photographic facsimile of the First Quarto.

William Shakespeare, *The Complete Works*, gen. eds Stanley Wells and Gary Taylor (Oxford: Oxford University Press, 1988).

### Q vs. F

Graham Holderness, *Textual Shakespeare* (Hatfield: University of Hertfordshire Press, 2003), contains many provocative forays into recent bibliographical controversies, as well as a chapter on

*Henry V* that nicely complements Patterson's *Shakespeare and the Popular Voice.*

Annabel Patterson, *Shakespeare and the Popular Voice* (Oxford: Basil Blackwell, 1989), offers a thorough reconsideration of the concept of 'bad quarto' and a fascinating account of F as Shakespeare's attempt to mediate in contemporary political issues.

## First productions

Andrew Gurr and Mariko Ichikawa, *Staging in Shakespeare's Theatres* (Oxford: Oxford University Press, 2000), a short, eminently useful account of the conditions of original staging.

## 2  The Play's Sources and Cultural Context

Phillipe Ariès, *The Hour of Our Death* (Oxford: Oxford University Press, 1991), a fascinating historical account of changing attitudes towards death.

Geoffrey Bullough (ed.), *Narrative and Dramatic Sources of Shakespeare*, vol. IV: *Later English History Plays* (London: Routledge and Kegan Paul, 1966), contains *Famous Victories* and all pertinent sections of Holinshed.

Caroline Walker Bynum, *Fragmentation and Redemption: Essays on Gender and the Human Body in Medieval Religion* (New York: Zone, 1991).

John Keegan, *The Face of Battle* (New York: Penguin, 1978), a superb look at battle from the standpoint of the individual in the midst of it, containing a detailed account of Agincourt.

Nigel Llewellyn, *The Art of Death: Visual Culture in the English Death Ritual, c. 1500–c. 1800* (London: Reaktion Books, 1991), explores attitudes toward death, the body and the soul.

Thomas Nashe, *Pierce Penniless: This Supplication to the Devil* (1592).

Annabel Patterson, *Shakespeare and the Popular Voice* (Oxford: Blackwell, 1989).

Alan Sinfield, *Faultlines: Cultural Materialism and the Politics of Dissident Reading* (Berkeley: University of California Press, 1992).

## 4   Key Productions and Performances

### General works

Ralph Berry, *Changing Styles in Shakespeare* (London: George Allen and Unwin, 1981), contains a still useful chapter on *Henry V* in performance.

Ralph Berry, *On Directing Shakespeare* (London: Hamish Hamilton, 1989), contains interviews with Adrian Noble and Michael Bogdanov.

Barbara Hodgdon, *The End Crowns All: Closure and Contradiction in Shakespeare's History* (Princeton, NJ: Princeton University Press, 1991).

James N. Loehlin, *Henry V*, Shakespeare in Performance Series (Manchester: Manchester University Press, 1996); of productions discussed in this section, Loehlin deals sensibly and thoroughly with the 1984 RSC and 1987–9 ESC stage versions; he also covers the Olivier, BBC and Branagh screen versions.

Emma Smith (ed.), *King Henry V*, Shakespeare in Production Series (Cambridge: Cambridge University Press, 2002); the best and most current stage history available, in narrative form in the introduction, and keyed alongside the text in a line-by-line commentary on distinctive production choices, cuts, business, etc.

### Specific productions

Michael Bogdanov and Michael Pennington, *The English Shakespeare Company: The Story of 'The Wars of the Roses', 1986–1989* (London: Nick Hern, 1990).

Michael Cordner, 'Repeopling the Globe: the Opening Season at Shakespeare's Globe, London 1997', in Stanley Wells (ed.), *Shakespeare Survey*, 51 (Cambridge: Cambridge University Press, 1998), pp. 205–17; lengthy reviews of the Globe's first season, including descriptions and consideration of audience reaction and involvement.

Russell Jackson, 'Shakespeare Performed: Shakespeare at Stratford-upon-Avon, 1994–5', *Shakespeare Quarterly*, 46 (1995), pp. 340–57; review of Warchus production.

Russell Jackson and Robert Smallwood (eds), *Players of Shakespeare* 2 (Cambridge: Cambridge University Press, 1988), contains an essay by Kenneth Branagh on playing Henry for the RSC in 1984–5.

Pauline Kiernan, *Staging Shakespeare at the New Globe* (Basingstoke: Macmillan, 1999), documents the experiments and discoveries associated with the 1997 production of the play that opened the reconstructed Globe; also contains short interviews with actors and directors from the first few seasons.

Cynthia Marshall, 'Sight and Sound: Two Models of Shakespearean Subjectivity on the British Stage', *Shakespeare Quarterly*, 51 (2000), pp. 353–61; study of the relationship between the verbal and visual, describing numerous instances in the 1997 Globe *Henry V*.

Robert Smallwood (ed.), *Players of Shakespeare* 6 (Cambridge: Cambridge University Press, 2004), contains an essay by Adrian Lester on playing Henry at the National in 2003.

'Intimate Magnificence', *The Economist*, 20 September 1997, pp. 97–8; review of the Globe's *Henry V*.

Stagework, www.stagework.org.uk/   This site is an online educational archive for the 2003 National Theatre production, containing production diaries, video clips of performance and clips of multimedia used in the show, actor interviews, etc.

## 5   The Play on Screen

### General studies

Michael Anderegg, *Cinematic Shakespeare* (Lanham, MD: Rowman and Littlefield, 2004), contains short, accessible accounts of Olivier and Branagh.

Michael Bogdanov and Michael Pennington, *The English Shakespeare Company: The Story of The Wars of the Roses', 1986–1989* (London: Nick Hern, 1990).

J. C. Bulman and H. R. Coursen (eds), *Shakespeare on Television* (Hanover, NH: University Press of New England, 1988), contains academic pieces and contemporary reviews of the BBC Shakespeare series.

Deborah Cartmell, *Interpreting Shakespeare on Screen* (New York: St Martin's Press, 2000), contains a brief but interesting chapter on the Olivier and Branagh film versions that ultimately finds Branagh's treatment even more conservative than Olivier's wartime effort.

Sarah Hatchuel, *Shakespeare, from Stage to Screen* (Cambridge: Cambridge University Press, 2004), contains a brief 'case study' of the wooing scene in the Olivier and Branagh films.

Russell Jackson (ed.), *The Cambridge Companion to Shakespeare on Film* (Cambridge: Cambridge University Press, 2000); good reference book, containing articles on adaptation, on directors Olivier and Branagh, and on critical issues such as nationality and women on film.

James N. Loehlin, *Henry V*, Shakespeare in Performance Series (Manchester: Manchester University Press, 1996).

Kenneth Rothwell, *A History of Shakespeare on Screen: A Century of Film and Television* (Cambridge: Cambridge University Press, 1999).

Emma Smith (ed.), *King Henry V*, Shakespeare in Production Series (Cambridge: Cambridge University Press, 2002).

## Olivier

Laurence Olivier, *On Acting* (London: Weidenfeld and Nicolson, 1986).

## Branagh

Kenneth Branagh, *Henry V by William Shakespeare: A Screen Adaptation by Kenneth Branagh* (London: Chatto and Windus, 1989); the introduction and staging directions give a clear sense of the 'interior life' and psychological imperatives guiding Branagh's filming decisions.

Benedict Nightingale, 'Henry V Returns as a Monarch for This Era', *New York Times*, 5 November 1989; interview with Kenneth Branagh prior to his film's US release.

## 6   Critical Assessments

### Overviews and collections of recent criticism

Michael Hattaway (ed.), The Cambridge Companion to Shakespeare's History Plays (Cambridge: Cambridge University Press, 2002).

Emma Smith (ed.), Shakespeare's Histories (Oxford: Blackwell, 2004).

R. J. C. Watt (ed.), Shakespeare's History Plays (London: Longman, 2002).

Stanley Wells and Lena Cowen Orlin (eds), Shakespeare: An Oxford Guide (Oxford: Oxford University Press, 2003).

### Specific works cited in this section

Joel B. Altman, ' "Vile Participation": the Amplification of Violence in the Theater of Henry V'. Shakespeare Quarterly, 42:1 (Spring 1991), pp. 1–32.

Howard Barker, Arguments for a Theatre, 2nd edition (Manchester: Manchester University Press, 1993).

Michael Bogdanov and Michael Pennington, The English Shakespare Company: The Story of 'The Wars of the Roses', 1986–1989 (London: Nick Hern, 1990).

Stephen Greenblatt, Shakespearean Negotiations (Oxford: Clarendon Press, 1988).

Nicholas Grene, Shakespeare's Serial History Plays (Cambridge: Cambridge University Press, 2002).

Barbara Hodgdon, The End Crowns All: Closure and Contradiction in Shakespeare's History (Princeton, NJ: Princeton University Press, 1991).

Jean E. Howard and Phyllis Rackin, Engendering a Nation: A Feminist Account of Shakespeare's English Histories (London: Routledge, 1997).

Pauline Kiernan, Staging Shakespeare at the New Globe (Basingstoke: Macmillan, 1999).

Jan Kott, Shakespeare our Contemporary (London: Methuen, 1965).

Tony Kushner, 'Ten Questions for Tony Kushner', New York Times, 4 June 2004.

Alexander Leggatt, Shakespeare's Political Drama (London: Routledge, 1988).

James N. Loehlin, Henry V, Shakespeare in Performance Series (Manchester: Manchester University Press, 1996).

Thomas Nashe, *Pierce Penniless, His Supplication to the Devil* (1592).

Norman Rabkin, *Shakespeare and the Problem of Meaning* (Chicago: Chicago University Press, 1981).

Phyllis Rackin, *Stages of History: Shakespeare's English Chronicles* (London: Routledge, 1990).

A. P. Rossiter, *Angel with Horns: Fifteen Lectures on Shakespeare* (Burnt Mill, Harlow: Longman, 1961).

Alan Sinfield, *Faultlines: Cultural Materialism and the Politics of Dissident Reading* (Berkeley: University of California Press, 1992).

Emma Smith (ed.), *King Henry V*, Shakespeare in Production Series (Cambridge: Cambridge University Press, 2002).

Alison Thorne, '"Awake Remembrance of These Valiant Dead": *Henry V* and the Politics of the English History Play', *Shakespeare Studies* (2002), pp. 162–89.

E. M. W. Tillyard, *Shakespeare's History Plays* (New York: Barnes and Noble, 1944).

Valerie Traub, *Desire and Anxiety: Circulations of Sexuality in Shakespearean Drama* (London: Routledge, 1992).

W. B. Worthen, *Shakespeare and the Force of Modern Performance* (Cambridge: Cambridge University Press, 2003).

# Index